D0208723

THE POWER OF STORY

Rediscovering the Oldest, Most Natural
Way to Reach People for Christ

LEIGHTON FORD
with James Denney

NAVPRESS
BRINGING TRUTH TO LIFE
NavPress Publishing Group
P.O. Box 35001, Colorado Springs, Colorado 80935

The Navigators is an international Christian
organization. Jesus Christ gave His followers the Great
Commission to go and make disciples (Matthew 28:19). The aim of
The Navigators is to help fulfill that commission by multiplying
laborers for Christ in every nation.

NavPress is the publishing ministry of The Navigators. NavPress
publications are tools to help Christians grow. Although publications alone cannot make disciples or change lives, they can help
believers learn biblical discipleship, and apply what they learn to
their lives and ministries.

Library of Congress Catalog Card Number:
        94-14344
ISBN 08910-98518

Some of the anecdotal illustrations in this book are true to life and
are included with the permission of the persons involved. All other
illustrations are composites of real situations, and any resemblance
to people living or dead is coincidental.

Ford, Leighton.
        The power of story : rediscovering the oldest, most natural
way to reach people for Christ / by Leighton Ford, with Jim
Denney.
                p.   cm.
        ISBN 0-89109-851-8
        1. Storytelling—Religious aspects—Christianity.
        2. Evangelistic work. I. Denney, James D. II. Title.
BT83.78.F67 1994
269—dc20   94-14344
                                                       CIP

Printed in the United States of America

FOR A FREE CATALOG OF
NAVPRESS BOOKS & BIBLE STUDIES,
CALL 1-800-366-7788 (USA)
or 1-416-499-4615 (CANADA)

CONTENTS

PART ONE: THE POWER OF STORY

CHAPTER ONE
The Story of God
9

CHAPTER TWO
Story: *They Met in Barcelona*
17

CHAPTER THREE
Toward 2000—and Beyond
25

CHAPTER FOUR
"Tell Us a Story"
35

CHAPTER FIVE
Story: *The Last Night in Barcelona*
53

PART TWO: THE LOVE OF GOD THE FATHER

CHAPTER SIX
A Generation in Search of Fatherhood
63

CHAPTER SEVEN
An Old Story for a New Age
75

CHAPTER EIGHT
Story: *Reunion in Atlanta*
89

PART THREE: THE GRACE OF THE SON

CHAPTER NINE
The Story Made Visible
99

CHAPTER TEN
A Touch of Grace
121

CHAPTER ELEVEN
Story: *A Skeptic Considers*
137

PART FOUR: THE FELLOWSHIP OF THE HOLY SPIRIT

CHAPTER TWELVE
In Search of Power and Community
145

CHAPTER THIRTEEN
The "Five-Finger Exercise"
159

CHAPTER FOURTEEN
Story: *A New Story Begins*
173

EPILOGUE:
The Story Goes on Forever
179

Notes
181

ACKNOWLEDGMENTS

Many people's stories are a part of this book. I'd like to say thanks for just a few. For my wife, Jeannie, our daughter, Debbie, and her husband, Craig, our son, Kevin, and his wife, Carly, whose stories have intertwined with mine. For the folks at Dallas Seminary who invited me to give lectures and listened so attentively as I gave the thoughts that have become this book. For Jim Denney with whom I have collaborated on the writing. And most of all to my God – Father, Son, and Holy Spirit—whose Story has touched my story for time and eternity.

PART ONE

The Power of Story

CHAPTER ONE

THE STORY OF GOD

*May the grace of the Lord Jesus Christ,
and the love of God, and the fellowship
of the Holy Spirit be with you all.*

2 CORINTHIANS 13:14

STORY → VISION → CHARACTER → EVANGELISM

Melvin Graham is the younger brother of Dr. Billy Graham. One Sunday morning, many years ago, Melvin was sitting at home, reading his Bible. For some time, he had felt completely overshadowed by his famous brother. In fact, he felt so inadequate as a Christian that he had stopped attending church.

Looking back on that time of discouragement, he recalls, "I couldn't witness, I couldn't speak publicly like my brother, I had no education to speak of—I just felt like a nothing."

As he was thumbing through his Bible, he happened upon the story of Moses in Exodus 4, where the Lord speaks from a burning bush and appoints Moses to be His spokesman. "O Lord, I have never been eloquent," objects Moses. "I am slow of speech and tongue."

Those words of Moses resonated like a clanging bell within the soul of Melvin Graham. That was *his* story! Moses was expressing *his* feelings! That story gave him a vision of how God wanted to use his life. Melvin Graham might not be Billy Graham, he might not possess the eloquent tongue of his brother, but Melvin Graham could offer to God everything he was and everything he had: his willingness, his obedience, and his responsive spirit.

The story of slow-of-speech Moses became Melvin's story, and Moses became Melvin's "patron saint." The story of how God empowered and used Moses became Melvin's personal vision, and that vision transformed his character. Ever since that day, Melvin Graham has been a faithful lay witness for Jesus Christ, and many people have come to Christ through his direct, unassuming witness.

Melvin Graham is a living example of a concept I call *narrative evangelism*. His life illustrates the essential blueprint of narrative evangelism.

THE STORY PRODUCES A VISION, AND THE VISION TRANSFORMS CHARACTER

It is *transformed character* that enables ordinary, tongue-tied Christians to become God's storytellers—people who share the good news of Jesus. The transformed character of Christian men and women is the key to world evangelization at the end of the twentieth century and beyond.

Each of us has a story—what I call "a story with a small *s*," the story of our own lives. At some point in our journey through life, our story collides with the Story of God—"the Story with a large *S*." God's Story calls our story into question. We must make a choice: either to reject the Story of God or to merge our story with His Story.

In John chapter 9, we have just such a collision of stories. Jesus and His disciples encounter a man who has been blind since birth, and Jesus heals this man. The man has no idea who has healed him. When the Pharisees ask him how he was healed, he replies, "The man they call Jesus" did it. But the Pharisees are not satisfied. They demand to know more. So what does the man do?

He tells his story!

He tells it simply, without adornment. He doesn't know theology. He hasn't been to seminary. He hasn't had any training in evangelism. He just tells what "the man they call Jesus" has done in his life. When the Pharisees demand that he explain how Jesus healed him, he replies, "I only know one thing: I was blind but now I see!"

That is his story. And this story produces a *vision* in this man's life. Later, when Jesus again encounters this man, Jesus asks him, "Do you believe in the Son of Man?"

"Who is he, sir?" the man says in response. "Tell me so that I may believe in him."

"I am he," replies Jesus.

And the man believes. His eyes are truly opened—not just his physical eyes but his spiritual eyes as well—so that he can see Jesus clearly. His story ("the man they call Jesus has healed me") has produced a vision ("Jesus is the Savior, the Son of Man"), and that vision has transformed his character ("I believe!"). Now he is a *storyteller.*

The Story produces a Vision, which then transforms Character, resulting in evangelism. This process—*Story* ⟶ *Vision* ⟶ *Character* ⟶ *Evangelism*—provides us with a clear, workable, biblical pattern for effective, natural witnessing.

God has not called every Christian to preach in stadiums or witness door-to-door or hand out tracts on street corners. But he has called every Christian to be a witness. Like Melvin Graham and the man born blind, every Christian can tell his or her story. We can share out of our own experience what God has done in our lives. When the Story of God has produced a vision within us of who God is and what He wants to do in our lives, our character will be transformed in such a way that our witness—the telling of our stories—will be a natural outgrowth of who we are, a result of the transformed character God has produced in us. We will not be able to keep from telling our stories, because we *are* our stories. When people encounter us, they will see the Story of God written upon our lives.

A STORY IN THREE DIMENSIONS

As we have moved into the 1990s and now approach not only a new century but a new millennium, I have spent a lot of time reflecting on what our focus should be as a Christian church seeking to reach the world for Jesus Christ. There have been three factors that the Lord has used to shape my thinking about evangelism in these past few years.

Factor 1: The Influence of Billy Graham

When I was a young man in Canada, Billy Graham came to speak to a youth rally that I helped organize. We expected a great response to his ministry, yet following his messages hardly any people came forward and made a decision for Christ. Seeing how discouraged I was by this lack of response, Billy came over, put his arm around my shoulder, gave me a hug, and said, "I believe God has given you a burden to see people come to Christ, and I'm going to pray for you. I think if you stay humble, God will use you."

Billy became a mentor to me. He went back to North Carolina and told his sister, Jeanie, about this young fellow he had met in Canada. Jeanie and I later met when we both attended Wheaton College in Illinois. We got married and I joined the staff of the Billy Graham Evangelistic Association. I sometimes joke that Billy couldn't fire me because I was married to his kid sister! But the truth is that those years I spent watching, talking with, and working alongside Billy Graham helped to shape my own character, my values, my goals, and my passion for evangelism. When I look at the heart of Billy Graham, I see someone who has lived his life with a goal of knowing God's heart, and of trying to have the same heart for lost people that our loving God the Father has.

Factor 2: The Death of Our Son Sandy

Sandy died during heart surgery in November 1981. He was a young man, a junior at the University of North Carolina, and he had his whole life ahead of him—a life that Sandy was planning to use in service to God. The pain of losing a child is a pain almost beyond imagining—yet God used that experience to give my wife, Jeanie, and me an even deeper desire to see Him raise up more young men and women for the cause of Christ.

Factor 3: The Rapid Rate of Change Taking Place in the World Today

The world is undergoing sweeping changes. The old generation, the old leaders, the old perspectives and paradigms and ways of doing things are passing away. A new generation is emerging, and that generation is reshaping the world in profound ways. A new generation of Christians is arising around the world, and they are asking, "How do we meet the challenges of this new world? How do we carry the changeless Story of God into a rapidly changing world?"

In response to these changes in the world and to these factors in my own personal experience, I have taken time to step back and reflect on what should be the new paradigm for evangelism for the 1990s and beyond. And I have been thinking about it in a *Trinitarian* way—in terms of the Trinity of the Father, the Son, and the Holy Spirit. So often we begin our paradigms with *humanity*, with our human-designed programs, with our human perspective on what people need (or want) to hear. As biblical Christians, however, I believe our starting point must not be with the human story, but with the Story of God Himself. So as I reflected on the task of reaching this world for Christ, I began by focusing on that great apostolic, Trinitarian benediction, "May the grace of the Lord Jesus Christ, and the love of God, and the fellowship of the Holy Spirit be with you all."[1] And what emerged as I reflected on that benediction and as I prayed was the concept of narrative evangelism, in which the Story of God creates a Vision, the Vision produces Character—and that character is the character of a Christian evangelist, a Christian witness.

The Story that creates our Vision and produces our Character is the Bible, that vast and sweeping narrative that discloses God's Story—the Story with a capital *S. Narrative evangelism* is the act of living and telling this Story to other people.

The term *narrative evangelism* may sound like something new—and in some ways, it is. Yet, in a real sense, the purpose of this book is not so much to introduce something *new* as to return to God's *original* vision for evangelism—the same pattern of evangelism that was used by Jesus Himself. I believe history is forcing the church to clear away the clutter of methods, programs, and techniques that have accumulated around our understanding of evangelism. Increasingly, we find that the old approaches no longer work, so we are being driven to reexamine our understanding of what evangelism means. If we once again examine the task of evangelism through the lens of Scripture, we can see the Story of God with new eyes.

You and I are privileged to occupy a critical moment in human history. This is a time of fundamental change and social restructuring, and I believe we in the church are also on the brink of participating in a new spiritual revolution in Christ. God is calling His people to see the world in a new way, and to awaken to the opportunities before us.

Throughout this book, I will tell you a story. It is a fictional story about three people of our times—people I call Ben, Darrell, and Judith. Although they are fictional characters, they are composites of people I may have met. In their stories, I believe you will recognize facets of people you know as well. As we explore the stories of Ben, Darrell, and Judith, we will witness the unfolding of the Story of God in three distinct dimensions:

- The love of the Father
- The grace of the Son
- The fellowship of the Holy Spirit

Our goal is to uncover the crystalline simplicity of God's Story (with a capital *S*). Once we see how we have become a part of that Story, we will better understand how to tell and model our own story (with a small *s*) to others.

Conversion, in the truest sense, is a collision of narratives. God's Story touches my story and your story, and a collision takes place. People encounter stories that call their own stories into question, and they are forced to consider: *What if my story isn't the whole story? How should I respond?* In the process of reconsidering their own lives, they become caught up in the Story of Jesus, and they are *changed.*

This is not a book of grand strategies for converting the world.

This is a book with a very simple theme, a very basic strategy. It is written to encourage the average layperson to tell his or her story, and in the process, to help spread the Story of God. This is a book for the person who says, "I want to be a more effective witness"; and it's also for the person who objects, "But I *can't* be an evangelist! I don't know how!"

If you have become a part of the Story of God, then you have a story to share with the people around you. They are eager to hear it. They are *dying* to hear it.

Any Christian can be a witness, an evangelist. And every Christian should.

My friend, you have a Story to tell.

CHAPTER TWO

STORY:
They Met in Barcelona

THE SUMMER OLYMPICS: JULY 1992

Two Americans sat at a table in a noisy, crowded bar. A Casablanca-style fan slowly rotated over their heads, stirring the sultry, smoky air.

"Look, Ben," one of them shouted above the hubbub, "you may be one heck of a great sportswriter, but you don't know diddly about politics!" The speaker was a lean, athletic-looking African-American. He was grinning, but his eyes were intense. He was clearly enjoying the challenge of a good-natured argument.

"Okay, Darrell," said Ben, a big, barrel-chested man of about thirty, with pale blue eyes and flamboyant red hair. "I'll grant you, Bush is down in the polls, but Bill Clinton is just riding a post-convention wave of euphoria right now. You just watch: By November, Bush will win reelection—and he'll win big."

"No way, man!" Darrell countered loudly. "Bush is history! Clinton's got it locked solid!"

"The election's over three months away!" objected Ben, taking a pack of Camels from his pocket and tapping a cigarette into his hand. "*Nobody's* got it locked solid." He lit up, then expelled a cloud of blue smoke into the already-dense air.

Darrell took a slow sip from his beer, then said, "You know, Ben, I didn't come all the way to Barcelona just to argue politics in a hot, stuffy bar."

"Oh?" said Ben, grinning. "Then let's argue something else. Let's argue about the Olympics."

"Well, that's more like it, my man!" said Darrell. "And I think I've got the perfect argument starter: the Dream Team."

"What about the Dream Team?"

"I don't see where the U.S. gets off sending a bunch of NBA all-stars to an amateur competition like the Olympics."

"You gotta be kidding me! Are you telling me that those athletes the Russians have been sending for the past few decades have been *amateurs?* They pay their athletes *plenty* so they can spend every waking moment training for the Olympics. By sending Magic Johnson and Larry Bird, we're just doing what the Russians and a lot of other countries have been doing all along: We're putting our best competitors on the field!"

"Ben, Ben! Don't you see how that corrupts the game? We're putting guys who earn millions in the NBA up against a bunch of backyard hoop-players from places like Costa Rica and Pakistan! Where's the sportsmanship in that?!"

"All we're doing is playing by the new FIBA rules! If we can't—" Ben stopped and did a double take. "Hey! Is that who I think it is?"

Darrell turned and looked in the direction Ben was pointing. A woman was just coming into the bar from the street entrance. "You know her?" asked Darrell.

"It's been a long time," said Ben, "and she's wearing her hair longer, but yes, I'm sure that's Judith."

"Man," said Darrell, "the lady sure looks upset about something."

Darrell was right. The woman definitely wore an angry, harried expression.

Ben cupped his hands over his mouth and called out over the

roar of the crowd, "Judith! Judith, over here!"

The woman heard her name and looked around. When she saw Ben, her eyes widened. Instantly, the angry expression vanished from her face, replaced by recognition. "Ben!" she called, wading through the crowd. "Ben, I haven't seen you since journalism school!"

Darrell scooted his chair aside, making room for one more at the table. Judith slid in between them.

"Darrell, this is Judith," said Ben. "Judith, this is Darrell. I first met Darrell when I did a feature on him for the L.A. *Times*. We ran into each other at the stadium this morning."

"Small world, huh?" added Darrell. "And you two know each other from journalism school?"

"Right," said Judith. "How long has it been, Ben?"

"Seven years?" said Ben, scratching his head. "No. Eight! Gee, you look terrific! What are you doing these days? I remember your ambition was to be the first woman VP for sports programming at a major network. Still pursuing your dreams?"

"Getting closer all the time," Judith replied. "I'm an assistant producer now." She was an attractive woman of about thirty, with dark brown eyes, billows of dark brown hair, and a confident, engaging smile. Bold red hoops dangled from her ears, matching the bold crimson of her lips and her dress. Outwardly, Judith exuded self-assurance, conviction, and control.

"Did you ever marry that guy you were dating?" Ben continued. "What was his name—?"

"Carl? No. That was about four relationships ago. I'm living with a wonderful guy now. His name is Gardner. He's a senior producer in the news division at my network. And what are you doing these days? As I recall, your goal was to be a feature writer with *Sports Illustrated*."

"I left L.A. last year and moved to Chicago," said Ben. "I write for the sports section of the *Trib*. I like it—but I still have my sights set on *SI*."

The waitress came and Judith ordered white wine. Then she turned to Darrell. "So Darrell, what are you doing at the Olympics?"

Darrell grinned. "Just gawking at the spectacle, along with sixty-five thousand other people."

"Darrell's being modest," Ben interjected. "He's a sprinter and a hurdler. He competed at Seoul in nineteen eighty-eight. If he hadn't pulled a hamstring the week before team trials in New Orleans, he'd have been in the hundred-meter event this morning."

"Really?" said Judith, quite impressed.

"Well, yeah, I think I could've made the cut," Darrell replied with a shy smile. "I took a bronze in eighty-eight, and I really wanted one more shot at the gold—but I guess it was just not to be."

"So what are you doing now, Darrell?"

"I'm a third-year law student at UCLA."

Judith's wine arrived, and she lifted the glass to her lips. "It must be hard to sit in the stands and watch the other runners," she said, "when you really want to be down there on the track."

"Yeah, it's hard—but I couldn't stay away."

"I know what you mean!" said Judith, her eyes alight. "There's never been an Olympics like this one! Do you realize this is the first Olympiad in twenty years that no country has boycotted or been banned from? I think it's wonderful! When you think about it, you realize that the Olympics isn't just about sports, it's about the *world!* The world is changing. Communism's falling apart. A new spirit of cooperation is emerging among nations, and this Olympiad is overflowing with that new spirit. It kinda gives me hope that the human race might just make it after all." She stopped and laughed self-consciously. "Well, I'll step down from my soapbox now!"

"No, no," said Darrell, "everything you said is right on! I'd never thought of it that way, but you're right. The world *is* changing in a fundamental way—and these Games symbolize that change."

"Say, Judith," said Ben, "not to change the subject, but what were you so mad about when you walked in here? You looked like somebody really torqued you off."

"Oh, that!" she said, shaking her head. "I just got fed up with being harassed on the street. I ducked into this bar to get away from the hassle. Boy, was I glad to see a familiar face!"

"Who was hassling you?" asked Darrell.

"A bunch of Christians handing out leaflets," Judith replied, grimacing. "You can't walk two blocks without half a dozen of these [expletive deleted] religious fanatics trying to convert you! Personally, I don't care what kind of garbage people want to believe, as long as they keep it to themselves. I just think religion is a private matter and shouldn't be hawked on street corners."

"Isn't that the truth!" said Ben, frowning and stubbing out his cigarette. "As someone once said, 'There oughtta be a law.'"

"There already *is* a law," Darrell genially interjected. "They call it the First Amendment. I thought you ladies and gentlemen of the press were supposed to be the guardians of free speech!"

A lively but good-natured argument on religious freedom ensued. When the next round of drinks arrived, the talk turned to the Olympics—and particularly to Carl Lewis's record-breaking performance on the 400-meter-relay team. And when the check arrived, the conversation took yet another turn—this time to the outrageous Barcelonese prices.

"My hotel stuck me in a room with paper-thin walls," said Darrell. "Like, there's no phone, no TV, and the nearest toilet is at the far end of the hall! And they're charging me five-hundred bucks a night!"

"The food prices are just as outlandish," said Judith. "The ham sandwich I had for lunch today was ten dollars plus tip!"

"A ham sandwich!" exclaimed Ben, grinning. "For a nice Jewish girl like you?"

"I'm *ethnically* Jewish," Judith explained. "I love my Jewish heritage, but I can sure do without all those religious rules."

"Well, since we've circled right back to the subject of religion," said Darrell. "exactly what *do* you believe in, Judith?"

"Nothing, mostly. There are things I *care* about. World peace. Saving the environment. But there's not much I believe in. Oh, I've been thinking a lot about the New Age. I've been investigating the goddess movement and Gaia, the Earth Spirit. And I've been talking to some of my friends who are plugged into spirit guides. But so far, I'm just browsing, not buying. How about you, Darrell? What do you believe in?"

"I don't know," Darrell replied, looking down into the dregs of his beer. "My mother was real religious. She used to drag me to church three times a week. It was your typical black congregation, with a lot of singin' an' shoutin' an' testifyin'. When I was a kid, I believed every bit of it—you know, stuff like there's a God who cares about you and listens when you talk to Him and answers your prayers. But when I was thirteen, my mother got cancer. I prayed every day, and I just knew God was going to make my mother get well. But she didn't get well. I haven't been inside a church since her funeral."

No one spoke for several long moments. Darrell continued staring into his glass. Ben gazed off at the ceiling fan, which turned round and round, slowly agitating the sultry air. Finally, Judith broke the silence. "I'm sorry to stir up bad memories. It must have been very hard."

Darrell looked up and smiled. "That was a long time ago. But you know, there are times when I wish I could believe in God again. I guess it's just a nostalgia for those days when life was a lot simpler. But sometimes I wish . . . I just wish there really was a God you could talk to and count on." He sighed and turned to Ben. "How about you, Ben? What do you believe in?"

"I believe . . . ," said Ben with a faraway, philosophical look in his eyes. "I believe it's Judith's turn to buy the next round of drinks." He shot a sly wink in her direction.

"Come on, Good-Time Charlie," said Judith, nudging Ben in the arm. "The man asked you a serious question. Spill your guts!"

"Yeah, funny man!" added Darrell. "What do you believe in?"

"I don't think about religion," said Ben, spreading his hands. "It just never enters my mind. I don't believe in God—but I don't *dis*believe in Him either. If there is Someone out there somewhere, then He leaves me alone and I leave Him alone. I guess that makes me an agnostic."

"Is that how you were raised?" asked Darrell.

"No. My dad was Irish Catholic—that's where I got my flaming auburn locks—and my mom was Methodist. She used to take me to Sunday school and Dad took me to catechism. By the time I was eight or nine, I'd had my fill of religion. I just refused to go to church anymore. And in all the years since, I never missed it." Ben's face broke into that cockeyed grin Judith remembered so well from their J-school days. But she also detected something hidden just behind those smiling pale blue eyes—an unspoken sadness. When Ben checked his watch, Judith sensed that he was looking for a way out of an uncomfortable conversation.

"Hey!" he said, "look at the time! Do you realize we've been sitting here talking for three hours?"

Judith checked her own watch. "Is it that late? And I'm producing an interview with Kim Zmeskal at six in the morning! I've gotta scoot!"

"Hey, this has been great!" said Darrell. "How about if the three of us get together for dinner tomorrow night?"

"I'm booked for the next three nights," said Judith, "but if you gentlemen are still in town Sunday evening, I know a place that serves terrific paella."

"I'll be in town as long as my MasterCard holds out!" said Darrell, grinning. "Come on. Ben and I will walk you to your hotel."

They got up and walked out of the bar together, pushing their way through crowds of revelers and sightseers on the Ramblas. Neither Ben nor Judith nor Darrell had any idea how important this night would be in their lives.

CHAPTER THREE

TOWARD 2000—AND BEYOND

A WORLD OF CHANGE

We have just met three people: Ben, Judith, and Darrell. Now the question that confronts you and me is: How will we reach these three people with the gospel of Jesus Christ? For that is the central question of this book: How will we carry out the task of evangelism in a world that has changed in a fundamental way from the world we once knew? How will we reach a generation that views the world differently than generations past?

In early 1992, my wife, Jeanie, and I underwent a shattering experience that, to me, symbolizes what is happening to our world: our street disappeared.

Back in 1963, we built our two-story dream house on a quiet, shady, dead-end street in Charlotte, North Carolina. Over the next thirty years, we built a lot of memories on that street. I remember watching our daughter, Debbie Jean, walking through our backyard as she started kindergarten at the old Sharon School. I remember watching our older boy, Sandy, playing football with his friends on Mrs. Porter's nearby vacant lot. Sometimes one of our neighbors would be driving by and would honk and cheer if Sandy snagged a long pass—or hoot if he dropped one. I remember the proud grin of our youngest, Kevin, the first time he rode his bike down that street without training wheels. In our house on that quiet, shady street, we raised our children and wrote our family history and played and prayed and learned life's lessons together.

But even while we were storing up memories on that street, waves of change were lapping at the strong brick walls of our home. A big shopping mall rose up within walking distance of our home—the first of many commercial developments that were to spring up and threaten to engulf our quiet little street. As the years passed, traffic increased, and our quiet little street wasn't so quiet anymore. But still we stored our memories—memories of joy, memories of sorrow—in that two-story, brick-walled treasure box. Within those walls, we could look around and remember that perfect day in May, when so many of our friends and family gathered there to celebrate the marriage of our daughter. And we could remember the day, just a few months later, when those friends and family members gathered once again to mourn with us the death of our son Sandy.

All around us, vacant land and old houses were disappearing as commercial developers bought up property and put up new office buildings. One cold winter morning, I left our house and went to the office. As I drove away, the house next door was standing just as it had for more than twenty years. When I returned home at the end of the day, that house was completely gone—not one brick standing on another. The bulldozer that had committed this act of demolition was still sitting there, gloating over the pile of dust and broken planks that littered the lot next to our home. Words can't describe the eerie feeling of pulling into my driveway and seeing only a rubble-strewn scar where my neighbor's house stood only hours before.

I got out of the car and walked over to the bulldozer operator. "Twenty-odd years ago," I told him, "I stood here and watched that house being built. Now it's gone."

"Yeah," the man responded with a shrug. "That's progress."

I don't know if that's progress or not, but it certainly is *change*. And before too many more months passed, Jean and I reluctantly sold our storehouse of memories to those engineers of "progress," the commercial developers.

Today that house is gone. The neighborhood is gone. We live in a different house. It's a comfortable home, and we still have our pictures and our mementos and our memories. And we are making new memories every day.

But Debbie and Kevin won't be able to take their children to a quiet, shady street and point to a two-story house and say, "That's the place I told you about. That's the house where I grew up."

I don't blame anyone for the disappearance of our little street. I can't fault the developers for wanting to make the "best use" of the land. There's a certain inexorable quality to this kind of change: When a quiet little residential area becomes surrounded by a large commercial area, the residential area is bound to get swallowed up sooner or later. But I can't help feeling sad for this little street, only a block long, that was born, became a neighborhood, and then died within the short span of thirty years.

In the movie *L.A. Story*, Steve Martin proudly announces to a visitor from Britain—the land of Stonehenge and Roman walls and Saxon castles—"This is Beverly Hills! Some of these houses are actually *twenty years old!*" I laughed at the movie—but I grieved when I thought of my own house. To me, the story of the change that came into our lives when we lost our quiet little street is a parable of the rootlessness of modern America. We have lost our sense of place, our sense of identity, and this loss has contributed to the alienation—and perhaps even the violence—of our lives. These losses, I believe, can be traced largely to the enormous *change* that has come into all our lives in the last few decades.

There is nothing so inevitable in life as *change*. And in these times, change is not merely constant, it is rapidly *accelerating*. Scientists estimate that the volume of information in the world doubles at a rate of once every ten years. On a graph, the expansion of information in our own century would look like this:

1900 ▮
1910 ▮
1920 ▰
1930 ▰
1940 ▰▰
1950 ▰▰▰
1960 ▰▰▰▰
1970 ▰▰▰▰▰
1980 ▰▰▰▰▰▰▰▰
1990 ▰▰▰▰▰▰▰▰▰▰▰
2000 ▰▰▰▰▰▰▰▰▰▰▰▰▰▰▰▰

Volume of Information = ▰▰▰▰▰▰

As information in the world increases, the world changes. And since the volume of information in the world is expanding at an *exponential* rate—doubling, then doubling that, then doubling that again—the world is also *changing* at an exponential rate.

A couple of decades ago, for example, it took about seven years to bring a new car design from conception to production. Today, however, a new design moves from conception to show-room in a mere two years. It is no longer acceptable for an automobile to spend the better part of a decade on the drawing board. Society and the tastes of the buying public change too rapidly, so automakers must bring out new designs at a much more rapid rate.

Even so, change in the automobile industry is slow compared to other, more high-tech industries. Industrial analyst Regis McKenna says one year in a high-tech field such as computers is like seven years in any other industry. He estimates that a patentable innovation takes place every thirty seconds in Silicon Valley.

We can see the effect of this rapid change in high tech simply by looking at the kinds of computers we have in our homes. Ten years ago, for example, a typical home computer was an Apple II with a 64K memory. Today, all the computing power of *ten* Apple II computers fits on a *single chip* in an Apple Macintosh or IBM PC. Today's home computers are roughly one hundred times as powerful as the old Apple IIs—and cost half as much. The next ten years are expected to bring even more revolutionary changes in computers—and in our world.

Society is changing, values are changing, and ways of perceiving reality are changing. In addition to the accelerating rate of change in technology, industry, and information, we are witnessing these fundamental changes:

- The end of the Cold War and of Communism.
- The rise of the global economy and the global mind-set.
- Increasing concerns about global, social, and economic survival.
- A fundamental shift in values and belief systems.
- The increasing polarization in our society—the "culture war."

If we want to reach people like Ben, Judith, and Darrell, we must speak to the times in which they live. Our story must be communicated with both a sense of *urgency* and a sense of *constancy*. Why urgency? Because we must be ready to move quickly, to adapt instantly, to respond to the changes taking place in our society and in the lives of the people we touch. Why constancy? Because people like Ben, Judith, and Darrell are feeling increasingly insecure and anxious. They are asking, "Where is a still, secure place in a changing world?"

You and I, along with Ben, Judith, and Darrell, are living between two worlds: the modern world and the *post*modern world. The modern world is dying. A new postmodern world is emerging, and people today already look at the world through postmodern eyes. While the gospel message has not changed in two thousand years, our way of communicating that gospel *must* change if we are to be effective as we approach the beginning of a new millennium. To reach Ben, Judith, and Darrell, we must understand how they think and feel and view the world.

What has happened to reshape the way today's generation looks at the world?

Answer: It all began with a snapshot of a star.

MODERN TIMES

On May 29, 1919, British astrophysicist Sir Arthur Eddington was in West Africa to photograph a total eclipse of the sun. Eddington's goal: to test the validity of Albert Einstein's recently proposed theory of relativity. If a photograph of the eclipse showed that the image of a certain star shifted during the eclipse, then Einstein was right. If the star was not displaced, then Einstein was wrong, and the seventeenth-century physics of Isaac Newton still held true.

It was overcast and drizzling when the eclipse began, and of the sixteen photographs Eddington shot, fifteen were obscured by clouds. But one photograph was clear—and it showed a star shifted slightly out of position. Einstein's theory was confirmed.

In his book *Modern Times*, historian Paul Johnson sets that date—May 29, 1919—as the end of the classical world and the beginning of the modern world. The theory of relativity completely overthrew the old assumptions of what constitutes reality. The implications of relativity include such ideas as:

- There is no such thing as a favored, absolute, objective point of view.
- Observations about reality depend upon who is making those observations; under certain conditions, subjective experience takes the place of objective measurements.
- Space and time are relative, not absolute, concepts; the speed of an object can cause space to expand and time to contract, or vice versa—depending on the point of view of the observer.
- Under certain conditions, the old Newtonian laws of cause and effect are no longer valid.

Even today, very few people understand these implications of Einstein's theory. The implications, however, have filtered from the scientific community through the intelligentsia to the media until they have become pervasive, impacting and saturating our culture's view not only of physical reality, but of ethics, morality, philosophy, and religion. As a result, the average person in the twentieth century now believes:

- There is no such thing as an absolute, objective point of view in matters of morality and religion. "You have your truth," people frequently say, "and I have my truth"—as if there is no such thing as *true* truth.

■ Subjective experience is just as valid as objective facts; we are free to invent any belief system we like according to what "feels right."

■ Truth and the nature of God are relative, not absolute concepts.

■ The old moral laws of cause and effect, of sin and consequences, are no longer valid.

From Eddington's day to our own, the basic structure of Einstein's theory of relativity has been confirmed again and again, in experiment after experiment. But it was a tragic, costly cultural mistake when philosophers took the scientific theory of relativity and extended it into the spiritual and moral arena. Moral relativism has cut the mooring lines of our society—and that is why we live in a world adrift. Einstein himself would have been horrified to find that his scientific theory of relativity has led to moral relativism—the belief that there are no moral or spiritual absolutes in the world. Although he was not orthodox in his beliefs, Einstein nevertheless believed that the world was created by a God who "does not play dice with the universe."

Relativity was the catalyst that gave rise to the modern mindset, but by Einstein's time there were already other streams of thought flowing from the nineteenth to the twentieth century, which were converging and changing the way people viewed their world. The four nineteenth-century thinkers who most profoundly changed the thinking of the twentieth century were Darwin, Freud, Marx, and Nietzsche, for they completely revised the way our century would think about society, power, and the human soul.

Charles Darwin gave us the theory of evolution by natural selection; he saw the world in terms of a struggle for survival, and his views on natural science were adapted by others and applied to society and economics under the label "social Darwinism." Sigmund Freud, "the Father of Psychiatry," published his *Essays on the Theory of Sexuality* in 1905, the same year Einstein published his special theory of relativity. Freud saw the world in terms of primal, animal, sexual drives. The ideas of Karl Marx, whose major work, *Capital* (*Das Kapital*), was published in the last half of the nineteenth century, became increasingly influential toward the turn of the century; Marx saw the world in terms of economic struggle. Friedrich Nietzsche despised Christianity and in his 1886 book, *Beyond Good and Evil*, he subjected the Christian faith and Western morality to relentless attack; Nietzsche saw the world in terms of the elevation of individual human power and will.

The net effect of these streams of thought was to create a new image of humanity and human existence. Whereas the old view of a human being was that of a creature made in God's image and occupying a meaningful place in God's creation, the modern view was that of an animal—highly evolved but ruled by deep primal drives; struggling for survival and dominance over his fellow animals; occupying a godless universe in which there was no right, no wrong, no absolute truth, no meaning.

Once this view of the world took hold in the early years of this century, what came next was inevitable: the rise of what Paul Johnson calls "gangster/statesmen." Once men began to discard moral boundaries and assert their own will to power, the stage was set for "a new kind of Messiah, uninhibited by any religious sanctions whatsoever. . . . The end of the old order, with an unguided world adrift in a relativistic universe, was a summons to . . . gangster/statesmen to emerge."[1] So the modern world summoned forth a deadly succession of nightmarish tyrants:

Come, Stalin . . .

Come, Hitler . . .

Come, Mao . . .

Come, Castro . . .

Come, Qaddafi . . .

Come, Pol Pot . . .

Come, Saddam . . .

And like specters riding out of the smoke of Apocalypse, they continue to come.

THE END OF HISTORY?

Just seventy years after the solar eclipse that confirmed Einstein's theory, something happened that brought a sudden end to the political arrangements of the modern world: the domino-fall of the Communist governments of Eastern Europe and the Soviet Union. The collapse of Communism was so swift that the Western world was taken by surprise.

The change that came upon the world at the beginning of the 1990s was so sweeping and profound that one U.S. State Department policy planner at the time, a man named Francis Fukuyama, wrote a much-discussed article called "The End of History." He observed that with the fall of Communism, "there is no longer any force except liberal democracy to win the world." Almost as an afterthought, he mentioned the fact that nationalism and religious fundamentalism (such as Islamic fundamentalism) still posed a minor challenge, but his net-net conclusion was that history was over. The superpower struggle was over. The threat of nuclear destruction was over. A truly *new* world order was at hand.

A few months after Fukuyama published these conclusions, Iraq invaded Kuwait. And then came civil war in the former Yugoslavia. And then came Somalia. Despite Fukuyama's hopeful (and, I think, naive) predictions, bloody human history marches on, driven to a large degree by the nationalism and religious fundamentalism that Fukuyama dismissed as an afterthought.

The postmodern world is an uneasy world. The sudden change in power structures, international alignments, and ideologies has created enormous uncertainty in the world. In a strange and somewhat perverse way, we had become comfortable with the clear-cut, us-versus-them alignments of the Cold War. But now that the Cold War is over, the issues that once divided the world into black and white, into good and evil, have become muddled and confused. And even though most rational people consider the collapse of Communism to be a good thing, if we are honest with ourselves we must confess to a vague sense of disquiet—an unsettled feeling caused by sudden, rapid *change* in the world.

We live in an axial moment of history. The world is pivoting on the very place we occupy in time. Change is happening so rapidly that, as Peter Drucker has observed, "No one can say that the past is prologue and predicts the future." How long this unique moment in history will last, or what will result from it, no one can say. But we can say this: The anxious mood of our times presents *all* Christians—not only pastors, evangelists, and missionaries, but ordinary believers in the pews as well—with a daring challenge and an unprecedented opportunity for modeling and telling the Story of God.

CHAPTER FOUR

"TELL US A STORY"

THE BROKENNESS OF EAST AND WEST

Gregory was looking for a yoga teacher.

It was 1991, and our Leighton Ford Ministries team was in Moscow, conducting training seminars for pastors. Gregory, a twenty-year-old student from Teacher's College, came to our hotel looking for a yoga teacher who could help in his search for spirituality. In the lobby, he met one of my companions. My colleagues and I couldn't teach him yoga, but we felt we had something of lasting value to offer him: the Story of God. Fortunately, we needed a guide to take us around Moscow that afternoon, so we hired Gregory.

As we traveled on the subway, we had a lot of time to talk. "Gregory," I said, "tell me about yourself. What do you like? What are you interested in?" It was fascinating to get a close-up look at the hopes and interests of a young man who had grown up behind the Iron Curtain. Like young people all over the world, he wanted a family, he wanted a good job, he wanted his life to count for something.

Finally, I said, "Gregory, what do you believe in?"

He said, "Nothing. The past was a lie. The present gives me nothing to build my life on. The future gives no hope for reconstruction of our society and our economy until my grandchildren's day, at the earliest."

I said, "Do you believe in science?"

"A little bit. Maybe."

"Do you believe in God?"

Gregory thought about that for a moment, and then he said, "Once, five years ago, I heard about God on the radio. The program ran for about three weeks, then it went off. I've always wished I could learn more."

We talked further as we toured the city. Gregory mentioned some physical problems he had been having, and for a moment I was reminded of my son Sandy, who was about Gregory's age when he experienced the heart problems that eventually took his life. At the end of our journey around the city, I gave Gregory an English Bible and a copy of my book *Sandy*. Since then, I've often thought about Gregory, about his sincere hunger for spiritual reality, and about his haunting words, "I believe in nothing. The past was a lie. The present gives me nothing to build my life on. The future gives no hope." Those are tragic, heartbreaking words.

And yet, as we look across the landscape of our world, viewing people as God views them, one fact becomes clear: The brokenness and emptiness of our world, both East and West, is our opportunity. Now more than ever before, people are ready to listen to our Story.

People who are comfortable tend to be complacent. But those who have become aware that their lives are empty, that their world is broken, are eager to hear our Story. And the foundations of this world *are* crumbling.

In his book *Christian Belief in a Post-Modern World,* Diogenes Allen lists four foundations of modern thought that are collapsing in this postmodern age and making our generation more receptive to the gospel Story. They are: (1) the intellectual assumption that the idea of God is superfluous as an explanation for the universe; (2) the belief that morality can be derived from reason instead of religion; (3) the belief that progress is inevitable; and (4) the belief that knowledge is inherently good. Let's examine each of these foundations in turn:

Foundation 1: The Intellectual Assumption that God Is Superfluous

In 1805, the French astronomer, the Marquis de Laplace, presented the first in his five-volume work on astronomy, *Celestial Mechanics*, to Emperor Napoleon. The emperor read the book carefully from cover to cover, then called for Laplace. When Laplace arrived, Napoleon said, "You have written a very lengthy book about the universe without once mentioning the Author of the universe." Laplace's reply: *"Je n'ai pas besoin de cet hypothèse"* (I have no need of that hypothesis).

In the two centuries since Laplace, the majority of modern-era scientists and philosophers have adopted the Laplacian position: God is no longer required as an explanation for anything. The existence of plant and animal life is explained by evolution and natural selection. The existence of the universe is explained by the big bang theory. The existence of matter is explained by quantum mechanics. So what do we need God for? The answer of the modern-era scientists: "We have no need of the God hypothesis."

However, new developments and discoveries in physics and cosmology are dragging modern-era scientists into the postmodern age. "In my opinion," writes astronomer Paul Davies, "science offers a surer path to God than religion."[1] And astronomer Fred Hoyle adds, "A commonsense interpretation of the facts suggests that a superintellect has monkeyed with physics, as well as chemistry and biology, and that there are no blind forces worth speaking about in nature."[2] The emerging evidence is forcing scientists to ask themselves, "Why does the universe have *this* order rather than another one? Why does the universe even exist?" Suddenly, the same scientists who once shrugged off the need for the "God hypothesis" are facing the uncomfortable fact that the evidence points to the existence of God.

The issue of whether God exists is important because human beings are goal-seeking creatures. Our needs, aspirations, and desires are far greater than can be satisfied by an empty universe. Instinctively, we all feel that there *must* be more to the universe than blind chance and dead matter—and the evidence of post-modern science agrees with our deep yearnings for transcendence and for God.

Foundation 2: The Belief that Morality Can Be Derived from Reason Instead of Religion

Ever since the Enlightenment of the seventeenth and eighteenth centuries, secular philosophers have been trying to find a way to devise an objective morality based on reason alone. It has become clear in our own culture that this effort has failed miserably. Our society is deeply divided over issues of basic morality. Sexual ethics, the sanctity of life, medical ethics, economic justice, criminal justice, and war and peace are just a few of the issues where we are unable to reach a consensus as a society. As traditional Judeo-Christian morality is pushed away from the center of our laws and our conduct, we are finding ourselves without any basis for discussing and deciding what is moral or immoral, what is right or wrong. As Diogenes Allen concludes, "We find ourselves increasingly in the time of the Judges, in which each does what is right in his or her own eyes."[3]

Foundation 3: The Belief that Progress Is Inevitable

The strides that have been achieved in science, technology, and medicine from ancient times to the present day have contributed to the modern belief that progress is inevitable. As a result, many people have cherished a parallel belief that if we could only learn enough and grow wise enough as a society, we could solve all human ills, sins, and misery. Progress in education and social reform would eventually produce a utopia. In postmodern times, however, we are seeing the breakdown of that belief. We are faced with our failure to eradicate crime, pollution, poverty, hunger, racism, and war. In this country, neither the Great Society nor trickle-down economics seems to have worked. And around the world, we see that technology and our increased knowledge are being used to produce more sophisticated instruments of torture, oppression, and warfare.

The rising use of terror tactics and indiscriminate slaughter—from the bombings of Dresden and Hiroshima to the genocide in Cambodia to the gassing of Kurds in Iraq—has caused greater death among civilians and children than among military combatants. Without question, our own twentieth century has proven to be the bloodiest in human history—a grim dress rehearsal for Armageddon. Despite our electronic gadgets, our increased life span, and our best intentions, utopia is no closer today than it ever was.

Foundation 4: The Belief that Knowledge Is Inherently Good
When the morality of the Judeo-Christian tradition was firmly in place, society could be assured that scientists would use their knowledge in ethical ways, for the betterment of the human race. Today we have no such assurances. It is clear that many scientists are willing to develop their technologies without regard to how those technologies will be used. Exotic weapons, genetic engineering, and information technologies with enormous potential for the invasion of our privacy are just a few of the uses to which scientific knowledge are being put. Many postmodern people see the possibilities that await them on the horizons of science—and they are justifiably scared.

As the foundations of the modern mind-set continue to crumble, the world increasingly becomes a frightening and insecure place. Postmodern people are searching for new directions and new answers. As a result of the confusion and disquiet generated by the swift change that has come upon the world, we now see postmodern people searching for the values and the hopes that vanished during the modern age. And that is our opportunity as Christians in a postmodern world: people need what the gospel offers—meaning, hope, and absolute truth. Despite the strong challenges that face us, the Christian Story has never had a greater opportunity for advance than it does *right now*.

THE GLOBAL PLAYING FIELD
In 1992, I was in Sinaia, Romania, to lead a Leighton Ford Ministries leadership conference for aspiring young men and women who wanted to evangelize their country. In all my years as an evangelist—

and I have been involved in evangelism since I was sixteen—I have never seen anything to compare with the hunger for the gospel that I saw in Eastern Europe after the fall of Communism.

At the hotel where we were meeting, a Romanian woman came in off the street to apply for a job. She heard music at the end of the hall, coming from our conference room. She came in, sat in the back, and listened to the hymns and choruses. After the singing, a German pastor got up and began to speak on the subject of homiletics—that is, on how to prepare and deliver a sermon. This Romanian woman sat at the back and listened to the whole talk, then at the end, during the question-and-answer period, she raised her hand. "I want to accept Jesus Christ," she said, simply and earnestly. So the pastor called her up to the front and led her to Christ right in front of all these young pastors-in-training.

This woman symbolizes the spiritual hunger that is sweeping not only Eastern Europe but the entire world, following the collapse of the modern world. The domino-fall of Communism, which marked the beginning of the postmodern age, has ripped the cover off a huge secret: People around the world are hungry for hope and for meaning. Hearts are ripe for the gospel. The opportunities are everywhere.

You may be thinking, *But I'm not a missionary! I can't go to Eastern Europe or to some other part of the world and tell God's Story over there! I've never been trained to do evangelism! I don't know the language! I have responsibilities and a mortgage and a job to do right here!*

My purpose in telling this story is not to persuade you to become an overseas missionary, but rather to give you a glimpse of what God is doing on the global playing field. God has a great global plan of evangelism, and you have a part to play in that plan, even if you never venture farther from home than the next block. You can perform that part right where you are—in your neighborhood, in your family, in your place of work. All around the world, and right within your reach, there are people who are hungry for the Story of God. Whether you are called by God to tell His Story in Moscow, Russia, or Moscow, Idaho, you will be a much more effective Storyteller once you see the big picture, the global picture, of the great evangelistic project that God is carrying out in the world.

Let's examine together a few of the new opportunities for evangelism that have emerged in the postmodern world of the 1990s.

The Islamic World

The greatest religious challenge to Christianity is Islam. The Muslim world stretches all the way from North Africa through the Middle East, through the Indian subcontinent, and out to Indonesia on the Pacific Rim. In fact, you could even say that the Muslim world stretches all the way to North America: Today, there are more Muslims than Methodists in the United States, and the number is growing. The Islamic faith is a much stronger competitor than Marxism ever was, because Marxism never had the spiritual commitment at heart that Islam does. Yet, despite the fierce dedication of the Islamic heart, God is at work, drawing Muslims to His Son, Jesus.

I recently received a report from an Islamic country in Africa.[4] A ship operated by a Christian missionary organization often docks in this country, offering people medical care and witnessing to the gospel. On one visit, the people from the ship brought together the Christian leaders of the country to pray that God would spread His Story throughout that Muslim nation. And God answered their prayer in an amazing way. In this one country, twenty-three Muslim *imams*—dedicated teachers of the Koran—had a vision of Jesus coming to them and saying, "Islam is not the way. I am the way. Follow Me." And these imams went to the Christian pastors and said, "Tell us about Jesus Christ."

This anecdote is not meant to suggest that Christianity is sweeping through the Muslim culture. There are still enormous obstacles to the gospel throughout the Muslim world. In fact, in many Islamic countries, Muslims can be imprisoned for changing their religion, and even for possessing Christian literature. There is a fierce antagonism against Christianity within most Muslim hearts— an antagonism dating back to the atrocities committed against Muslims in the name of Christ by the Crusaders of the Middle Ages. That is why it is important, when we witness to Muslims, to present Christ as a Person, *not* Christianity as a system.

The challenge is great—but the power of God is even greater. Do we believe in the power of God to make sweeping, dramatic changes in the world? After the fall of Communism, can't we place our trust in a God who holds all of history in His hands? For decades, we Christians have made the mistake of writing off the Muslim world. We have said, "The Muslim culture is closed. The Islamic people are completely unreceptive to our gospel." But in these postmodern times, God wants to give us a new vision and a heart full of compassion for the Muslim people.

In Acts 10, God simultaneously gave a vision to a pagan named Cornelius and to a Christian named Peter, then God brought them together so that Peter could share the Story of God with Cornelius. Today, we see that God has given a vision of Himself to people in the Muslim world—and He has set a vision before us. The question is, Will we, like Peter, obediently respond to that vision and reach out to the Muslim people who are hungry for the spiritual reality of Jesus Christ?

Eastern Europe and Russia

I was in East Berlin in the summer of 1988. There, one of the high-ranking leaders of the Baptist church in Communist East Germany told me, "Leighton, don't be concerned about Communism. In ten years, there will be no more Communism." I laughed inside. I thought, *This poor man lives under Communism and has no idea how monolithic it really is.* Yet by November of the following year, the government of East Germany had fallen, the Berlin Wall was open and crumbling, and German reunification had begun. My East German friend clearly understood what I failed to see: Communism, like a strong man, could be bound. My friend knew that there were not only empty shelves in the stores, but empty souls in the people. It only took a single push to send the entire Communist system toppling like a row of dominoes.

The fall of Communism created an enormous vacuum in Eastern Europe and Russia. There is a fierce competition among many global forces to fill that vacuum. I recently talked to the deputy director of philosophy at the Academy of Sciences in Moscow, and he said, "Dr. Ford, since the fall of Communism, we have opened up a connection with the West—but it's with the *sewer system* of the West. We are receiving American television, movies, violence, materialism, pornography, drugs, and all the rest of it. But we are spiritually empty, and we are not receiving from the West the things that fill our souls."

This statement tells us something about the emptiness at the core of Russian culture under Communism. But it also tells us something about our own culture. It tells us that the United States—this "one nation under God"—is busily manufacturing moral and spiritual "sewage," and exporting it around the world. It tells us that there is something fundamentally wrong with our own society. The fall of Communism has made it more clear than ever that it is time to critically reexamine our own nation and its values.

The United States of America and Canada

I am a U.S. citizen—but I haven't always been. I was born in Canada and was naturalized in 1991. The day I was to take the oath of citizenship, my grandson—who was six years old at the time—was excited because he was going to get to see me become an American citizen. He called my wife, Jeanie, and—using his terms for grandma and grandpa—said, "Mimi, you know what? I'm going to go see Gagee become a Christian!"

My grandson was only making the same mistake many of us Christians in the United States make today. We think we live in a Christian nation, and we equate being an American with being a Christian. We are reluctant to acknowledge one of the most profound changes that has taken place in our century: *the death of Christendom*. In fact, the U.S. has become so thoroughly secularized that it no longer makes logical sense to call ourselves "one nation under God."

Once we admit to ourselves that we live in a secularized society, another fact becomes clear: North America is now the largest mission field in the English-speaking world. And the 200-million-plus "secular" North Americans make the United States and Canada the third-largest mission field in the world—after China and India (although, of course, Americans have far more access to the gospel than people in many other parts of the world). These shocking facts open up an enormous range of opportunities for us! True, as Christians we do not enjoy a "home-field" advantage. We are playing on the opponent's field. And it may be threatening to us to realize that we Christians are now a minority movement even in the United States and Canada.

But let's look at our situation from God's perspective. In a real sense, we are back in apostolic times. We are in a missionary situation in our own countries, just as the early Church was. It is at times like these—when Christianity has become the minority view, and when the world has become an unsettled and frightening place—that the Christian church has historically made its greatest impact upon society. As in New Testament times, our "apostolic" postmodern North American church faces two difficult obstacles: (1) compromise from within and (2) opposition from without. Let's take a closer look at each of these obstacles:

Compromise from within. To be effective, we in the church must speak with a clear, resounding voice—a voice that is distinct from the cultural babble that surrounds us. Unfortunately, the church in many quarters has lost its distinct voice. When the church speaks, it all too often sounds like the rest of society. Why? *Because the church itself has been heavily affected by secularism.* The church has compromised with the surrounding society. Just like the secular world around it, the Christian church places a heavy emphasis on success, and it measures that success in numbers and in dollars. Our approach to church growth is too often dominated by marketing techniques and consumer standards. We believe that with better techniques, better programs, better hardware, we can do a better job at doing God's work. We, the church in North America today, need to subject ourselves to intense self-examination and honest self-criticism—and we have some repenting to do.

Opposition from without. The 1990s have brought a rapid upswing in opposition to Christians, to Christian values, and to the Christian Story. Now, more than at any other time in American history, the Christian gospel is being forced to compete in the marketplace of ideas. The competition is fierce and it is hostile. There is a culture war going on around us—a battle to determine who defines the values that really matter. Those who espouse a belief in "pluralism" and "multiculturalism" will be quick to attack Christians as "intolerant," "chauvinistic," and even "fascist," because Christians claim to possess a Story that is absolutely true. In the face of such attacks, we must be *bold* yet *gracious*. By "bold," I mean that we must never compromise the truth of our Story, nor hesitate to tell it whenever the opportunity arises. By "gracious," I mean that we must never allow our boldness to harden into brashness.

At one of our Leighton Ford Ministries seminars for young leaders, we had a discussion on the difference between being bold and being brash. One student came up with a good definition for these two words. *"Boldness,"* he said, "means I overcome *my* fears in speaking the gospel. *Brashness* means I am insensitive to the fears and anxieties of *others*." To be effective witnesses in a postmodern world, we must learn to listen to the concerns and needs of other people even as we boldly speak the truth of the gospel.

And that brings us back to our friends, Ben, Judith, and Darrell. To reach them with the Story of God, previous evangelistic approaches will no longer be as effective as they once were. Ben, Judith, and Darrell belong to a new and unique generation—a generation that has been called "Generation X," the "baby buster" generation. To reach them we will need to listen to them and to understand how they think and how they feel.

GENERATION X

The baby boomer parents of Ben, Judith, and Darrell were born during the time of rapid population increase (or "boom") following World War II and continuing to the early 1960s. But our three friends and their "baby buster" peers were born after the U.S. birthrate began to decline (or "bust"), due to the greater availability of contraceptives and abortion from the mid-1960s to the present. The history, values, and perspective of the busters are markedly different from those of their parents, the boomers.

In October 1993, a conference on baby busters was held in Charlotte, a joint effort of Leighton Ford Ministries and InterVarsity Christian Fellowship. Among the presenters at that conference was my son Kevin, who has spent many months conducting focus groups and researching the unique characteristics and mind-set of the buster generation.

> I'm a buster myself, [says Kevin,] so the research I did served in part to confirm and explain attitudes and perceptions I've seen within myself and my peers.
>
> Who are the baby busters? We are a worried, insecure generation. The two defining characteristics of our worldview are *survival* and *risk*. Coming out of college, we are less confident than the boomer generation that taking an entry-level job is the path to the American dream. We wonder if our career will still be there five, ten, fifteen years down the road, so we are much likelier than our parents to take the entrepreneurial route rather than the corporate route in search of success and security.
>
> We tend to think that the world has yanked the welcome mat out from under us. We feel—whether rightly or wrongly—that we don't have the advantages and opportunities that our parents had. We see the world as tougher, more competitive today than in decades past. We feel there are too many hoops for us to jump through, too much red tape to contend with, too much complexity, too many demands—and at the end of it all, no assurance of a payoff.
>
> We don't trust authority, because the authorities in our lives—parents, government, employers—have broken their promises to us. We don't respect rules or believe in absolutes. Our boomer parents gave us few boundaries at home. We see government and industry continually flouting the rules. We see that the people who break the rules are the ones who get ahead, and those who obey the rules find it harder and harder to survive. So when the people in my generation bump up against any rules, they are increasingly inclined to *break* those rules—as a matter of survival, from their point of view.
>
> The people of my generation have no memory of the Great Depression or World War II. Even the Watergate

crisis and the double-digit inflation of the Carter years are ancient history to us. So perhaps we lack perspective on what the word *crisis* really means, in a historical sense. As a result, we look around us and we see ourselves as a generation in crisis. We see ourselves as inhabiting an economic crisis, an environmental crisis, a social crisis of broken families and unloved children, and a crisis of failed leadership.

We are a self-absorbed generation. We are more concerned with how we look than what we know, think, or feel. For many of us, our drug of choice is body-altering steroids rather than mind-altering hallucinogens. We work out at the gym and wear hundred-dollar Air Jordan shoes even though we can't afford health insurance. We are more concerned with image than reality, with style rather than substance.

We are pessimistic. We spend a lot of time in introspection, a lot of time licking our wounds. We live dangerously. We are preoccupied with death. We wear black. We commit suicide.

We are impatient. We are always looking for the quickest, most expedient way to get it done. We don't write letters. We use voice-mail and electronic mail. We don't go to the library, we search a computer data base. We demand instant gratification.

Above all else, we expect to be entertained. We've grown up having plenty of money for Nintendo games and movies. Our boomer parents paid our bills and gave us plenty of extra money for fun. If it isn't fun, we don't want to do it. We take six or seven years to get through college so we can have plenty of time for fun along the way. We make career choices based on what will be fun. After graduation, we take a year off to go to Europe or Australia—to have some fun before we have to face the "real world."

When it comes to God—well, who knows? All religions are equally valid, right? "Different roads, same destination"—that's our creed. We busters don't like controversy, we want to maintain harmony, we don't want to appear "intolerant" or "rigid," so our belief system tends to be fuzzy, even wishy-washy. Besides, we're put off by the institutional church, with all its rules and its repressive morality. We distrust the church just as we distrust *all* institutions. Like every other institution of our society, the church institution has broken its promises to us. And yet—

And yet we busters want to believe. We want to have hope. We long to have faith that there is something beautiful and enduring beyond this life, that there is Someone out there in the universe who cares what happens to us, who hears us when we are hurting and helpless. We don't want to be alone.

But we don't want a faith that is nothing but rules and theology and meaningless ritual. We want a faith that works in the real world, a faith that is practical and makes a real difference in life.

From this picture that Kevin has painted, it's easy to see how the people of Generation X, the baby buster generation, differ from previous generations. We can also see from this description of an impatient, pessimistic, amusement-centered generation why the old evangelistic approaches won't work.

But what *will* work? How can we communicate the timeless gospel of Jesus Christ to the baby buster generation in such a way that they will listen to *our* Story—and make it *their* Story?

"The church will have to change the way it communicates," Kevin replies. "We baby busters relate to communication forms that are functional and minimalist. Don't give us the gray, boring pages of the *New York Times*. We want *USA Today!* Don't give us a documentary on PBS. We want our MTV! When you speak to us, keep it clean and simple, nouns and verbs, not a lot of adverbs and adjectives. Give us pictures, graphics, color, motion, sound. Above all, if you want to make a point, don't give us a lot of dry content—*tell us a story!*"

Narrative evangelism—the telling of the Story of God—is the key to reaching the hearts and minds of Generation X.

A NEW VISION

The end of the Cold War toppled us into the postmodern era before we even understood what was happening. Amid the euphoria of watching the collapse of the "evil empire," there was an understandable temptation for us in the West to cheer and say, "We won!"

But what did we win?

Looking around us, we can see how the collapse of Communism has made a visible impact on our economy. We are witnessing the mass closings of military bases, major dislocations in the defense industry, and the loss of many high-paying jobs. These are all visible effects of the fall of Communism.

But I believe the *invisible* effects are even more profound: We have experienced a *loss of national purpose* in the U.S. I wonder if we realize how much our focus as a nation, these past fifty years, has been on the containment of Communism. Now that Communism is no longer there, we have to ask ourselves, "What are we here for as a nation?"

In much the same way, I also wonder if we Christians in the West realize how much our motivation for evangelism and missions has been the containment of Communism. Why has church attendance remained comparatively high in the U.S., compared to the steady decline we have seen in other Western democracies such as Canada, Australia, and England? One of the reasons: For years we have said to ourselves, "Communism is the enemy! We have to evangelize to hold back Communism!" But that was *never* a biblical motive for evangelism and missions.

The "new world order" of the postmodern age has set before us a formidable challenge: to critique our own society and our own church, and to *redefine our purpose for evangelizing*. In other words, we need a new *vision* for evangelism—a vision that is responsive to the realities of the new world we live in.

What do we mean by "vision"? I would use the words *vision* and *paradigm* interchangeably. When we talk about a "new vision for evangelism," we are talking about the same kind of event that takes place periodically in science.

Scientists have their "vision" or "paradigm" of reality, which is based on an interpretation of scientific facts. As more and more facts are gathered, scientists sometimes come to the realization that a given paradigm or vision of reality does not fit all the facts. The standard interpretation of reality does not work as well as it used to, or does not go far enough. Older scientists tend to keep stretching and contorting their paradigm to make it fit those vexing, irritating new facts. But at about the same time, a younger generation of scientists arises—a generation that has not invested decades of time, effort, and emotional involvement in the old paradigm. These younger scientists propose a new paradigm, a new interpretation of the facts, a new vision of reality. The old paradigm is shoved aside while a new vision takes its place.

We saw this happen when Einstein's paradigm replaced Newton's paradigm. Many physicists of Einstein's day, who were schooled in the old paradigm of Newtonian physics, scoffed and ridiculed this mind-stretching new vision of relativity. But it was Einstein's vision that was confirmed in 1919—and the scientific vision of reality was never the same again.

We have reached a similar point in evangelism. We have our traditional ways of doing evangelism, but many of us are beginning to realize that the old paradigm of evangelism isn't working like it used to. "We know the gospel is true," we say, "but we don't seem to be able to reach our friends, our neighbors, or our coworkers with the old approaches. Our traditional methods of evangelism don't work as well as they once did, because the world has changed." So what is our response? Should we keep trying to patch up our old, worn evangelistic paradigms in the hope of keeping them running? No. There is only one reasonable response to the frustration and dissatisfaction we are experiencing with the old paradigms. We must find a *new* paradigm.

The moment of "Aha!" is at hand. Out of our frustration and spiritual unrest, a new vision of evangelism is emerging. As a result, we now have unprecedented opportunities to evangelize our workplaces, our neighborhoods, and our world by communicating and modeling the Story of God—*if we have the courage to change our approach*.

Can we adapt? Can we change? Are our eyes open to the new

vision for evangelism that God is setting before us in the post-modern age?

Tradition-bound programs are too slow, too late for a generation that is moving at the speed of light across the landscape of our world. Time is the new competitive arena. We cannot afford to take years to analyze trends and develop long-range strategies. We need to be quick and flexible enough to meet the challenges of rapidly changing situations and a rapidly moving generation. Bob Wong, president of Micro-Tek International, offers advice that is just as valid for Christians as it is for the business community: "For success in the '90s, you don't need to be big. You just need vision and the ability to move fast."

Of course, speed, flexibility, and adaptability *should* have been the benchmarks of our evangelistic efforts all along. These, after all, are the benchmarks of the Apostle Paul, who counsels us to live "not as unwise but as wise, making the most of every opportunity, because the days are evil."[5] And these are the benchmarks of the Lord Himself, who urged His followers to move quickly and decisively in their urgent mission of spreading His Story: "Do not take a purse or bag or sandals; and do not greet anyone on the road."[6] Jesus was sending His disciples on a mission of extreme urgency—and His mission for you and me is no less urgent. To be effective in the 1990s and beyond, the church must shed all the old baggage that has slowed it down. We must become the church that travels light.

True, we want to act wisely, not impetuously. But all too often, the tendency of the church is to stay mired in analysis long after the time has come to *act*. New, innovative forms of ministry are emerging every day (we will look at some of these in coming chapters). We must be bold enough, flexible enough, and decisive enough to seize the moment and use these innovative new tools of ministry to more effectively spread the Story of God across the face of our world.

HOW DO WE COMMUNICATE GOD'S STORY TO PEOPLE LIKE BEN, JUDITH, AND DARRELL?

Throughout this chapter, we have laid a historical foundation for everything that follows. We have taken a brief look at the cultural

forces that have produced our postmodern age and the generation—Generation X—that has inherited this age. We have examined the strategic placement of the Christian church at this pivotal
moment in history. Now it's time to tie all these strands back to
the central focus of this book: narrative evangelism. After consid-
erable study, prayer, and contemplation, I have come to the conclusion that narrative evangelism is the new paradigm for evangelism in the postmodern age. It is simple. It is biblical. It is
practical. And it is endlessly adaptable.

You—an individual Christian layperson, without any special
training or skills—can be a "narrative evangelist" in your own family, neighborhood, workplace, campus, dorm, or apartment complex.
You can be an effective teller of the Story of God right in the place
where God has put you.

Throughout the rest of this book, we will explore together the
three dimensions of the Story of God:

- The love of the Father
- The grace of the Son
- The fellowship of the Holy Spirit

Through practical examples and real-life stories, we will see how
each of these three dimensions of God's Story has a special relevance to the needs of postmodern men and women.

People like Ben, Judith, and Darrell.

CHAPTER FIVE

STORY:
The Last Night in Barcelona

THE SUMMER OLYMPICS: AUGUST 1992

"Judith's really late," Ben grumbled, puffing on a Camel as he paced. "Maybe she forgot."

"Relax," said Darrell, checking his watch. "She'll be here. It's only eight-fifteen. She probably got hung up doing some editing or something." They were in the lobby of Estrada's, a crowded, lavishly decorated restaurant just off the Ramblas.

"She forgot," he said flatly, exhaling a blue billow of smoke.

"Man, are you wound up! Somethin' botherin' you, Ben?"

Ben looked up sharply. "Me? No, I'm fine, fine, just fine. I just want to sit down and eat, that's all."

"You sure? You look kinda . . . hey, there she is!"

Ben turned, and sure enough, Judith was entering the restaurant with a stack of papers in her hand. "Hi!" she said breezily. "Sorry, I'm late."

"Late?" said Ben, ostentatiously checking his watch. "I didn't even notice. Hey, waiter! Waiter!"

"Let me, Ben," said Judith. "They know me here." She raised a finger to a Spanish gentleman in a tuxedo and black tie. *"Camarero! ¿Está lista nuestra mesa?"*

The man smiled broadly. *"Ah! Senorita! Venga con mi, por favor!"*

As they were shown to their table, Darrell pointed to the sheaf of papers in Judith's hand. "What're those? They look like—"

"Uh-huh," said Judith with a sigh. "More tracts from those religious nuts on the street. I got tired of saying no, so I just took what they handed me and went on my way. It was easier than fighting them." She unsnapped her purse, tossed the unwanted papers inside, and snapped it shut. "I'll dispose of these later."

"Hang on to that stuff, Judith," said Ben, grinning. "You've got enough literature there to start your own street-corner religion."

The waiter seated them and they ordered drinks, then pondered the selections on the menu. Ben looked puzzled. "What kinda food *is* this?" he asked after a few moments. "I don't recognize *any* of this stuff!"

Judith looked up from her menu. "It's *Spanish*, Ben. We *are* in Spain, you know."

"But where are all the things I like? Where are the chimichangas and the enchiladas and the chili rellenos?"

Judith rolled her eyes. "That's not *Spanish* food, Ben! That's *Mexican* food!"

"Oh. I thought it was all the same. I could sure go for some tacos and jalapeno salsa right now."

Judith looked flabbergasted. "Ben," she said, "are you telling me you've been in Barcelona all this time and this is the first time you've eaten in a *Spanish* restaurant? What have you been living on?"

Ben shrugged. "Pizza. McDonald's. And there's a great little Chinese place around the corner from my hotel."

Judith groaned.

Ben turned his menu around and pointed to an item. "Hey, Judith, what's that?"

"Trepas con jamón? That's honeycomb beef tripe. They slow-cook the tripe for twenty-four hours, then serve it with peppers and minced ham."

"Is tripe what I think it is?"

"If you have to ask, then it's what you think it is."

"Ugh. . . . Gee, Judith, I dunno what to order."

"Let me order for you, then." The waiter returned with the drinks and Judith ordered for the whole table—green tomato gazpacho and paella, plus assorted appetizers.

Darrell took a long, slow pull from his beer, then set his glass down. There was more than a touch of melancholy in his eye as he said, "Well, the Games are almost over. Just a couple more days and it's back to the States and the same old grind."

"Well, covering the Olympics *is* my grind," said Judith, "but it's an exciting grind. These Games have been amazing. This is the first time I've seen world records set with my own eyes! Did you two see that incredible performance by Kevin Young on the four-hundred-meter hurdles?"

"Tell me about it!" Ben exclaimed. "First man to break forty-seven seconds! Took the record away from Edwin Moses! You know, Judith, that was Darrell's event—before he pulled that hamstring."

"Really?" said Judith, turning to Darrell. "The injury must have been an awful disappointment. All those years of hard work and training."

Darrell shrugged. "Hey, I'm not in the same league with Kevin Young."

"You're always selling yourself short, Darrell," Ben countered. "Judith, I've seen this man run, and ol' Darrell here was a blinding streak. He flew like the wind over those hurdles. I think he had a real shot at the gold."

"You know," said Judith, "it occurs to me that our network may have missed a big part of the story of this Olympics. I mean, we covered the triumphs, the medals, the records—but we didn't do one story on the disappointments. And there were a lot of heartbreaking disappointments in these Games."

"Yeah," said Ben. "You may have something there. 'The agony of defeat' and all that. Like when Michael Johnson got aced out of that two-hundred-meter qualifier because of a lousy virus. And Dan O'Brien getting knocked out of the decathlon—another virus.

And Darrell here, aced out of team trials by a pulled hamstring."

"And there's Sergei Bubka from the Unified Team," said Judith. "He was everybody's pick to win the pole vault, yet he didn't place, didn't even clear his opening height. How do you figure that?"

"Fate turns on a dime, man," said Darrell. "You train and sweat and bust your hump for years, and your whole focus is on a few moments of glory on a dirt track. You get the flu, you pull a muscle, you have a bad day, who knows? It can all go up in smoke"—he snapped his fingers—"like *that*."

"How did you deal with the disappointment, Darrell?" asked Judith.

"Me?" Darrell shook his head. "I'm afraid I didn't deal with it very well. The ninety-two Games were all I was living for. And three weeks before team trials, it was ripped away from me. I went into a mean depression—really heavy. I started usin' blow—you know, cocaine powder. I mean, that's how crazy I was, 'cause I haven't used drugs since I was a kid. My body's a temple, you know? But I was so bitter, man! I was even mad at God! And I don't even *believe* in God!"

Judith tossed her head and laughed. "Isn't that the truth! Sometimes it seems like we need to believe in God, if only to have Someone to blame when things go wrong!"

"But let me tell you," Darrell continued, "I saw a guy this week go through a similar kind of disappointment. And the way he dealt with it—man, it just blew me away!"

"Who's that?"

"Dave Johnson."

"Oh, right!" said Ben. "I did a story on him when I was with the L.A. *Times*."

"Yeah," said Darrell, shaking his head sadly. "The guy was a shoo-in for the gold in the decathlon—and then he got that stress fracture and had to settle for a bronze."

"I was watching that performance," added Ben. "It was incredible. You could see the agony on his face during the hurdles and the long jump, but he just kept on going, straight through the pain. Hey, you know Johnson personally, don't you, Darrell?"

"Yeah," replied Darrell. "Our paths have crossed a few times.

In fact, I used to go over to the Azusa Pacific track and work out with Dave. I got a chance to talk to him yesterday. You know, after everything he's been through in the last few days, all he was concerned about was *me* and how *I'm* doing! Can you believe that?"

Judith leaned forward. "And guys, did you know what Dave Johnson did before he became a runner?" she said. "He was a gang member!"

"What?!" said Darrell. "Are you sure?"

"I produced a segment on him for the network," she replied. "It was a great interview. Right on camera, he said, 'Running from the police is what made me fast!'" She laughed lightly, and Darrell and Ben grinned. "Before he got his life turned around," she continued, "Johnson spent a lot of his spare time breaking into houses. Once, he and some of his buddies even stole five-thousand-dollars worth of beer from a warehouse!"

"No lie?" Darrell said doubtfully. "That doesn't sound like the same Dave Johnson I know. What turned him around?"

Judith spread her hands. "He says he's a 'born-again Christian' now."

Darrell scratched his head. "I guess religion really works—for some people, anyway. Whatever it was that changed him, he sure got his life straightened out. And I respect that."

Dinner arrived, beginning with green tomato soup and a plate of appetizers: fried squid, small fried fish, and finger sandwiches stuffed with Spanish chorizo. Ben watched in dismay as Judith picked up one of the crispy little fish and popped it whole into her mouth.

"You eat the whole thing?" said Ben, grimacing. "Head and all?"

"Of course," said Judith. "They're called *bocarones*. Just toss 'em in your mouth like popcorn! They're great!"

Ben pointed to the fried squid. "And did you have to order food with *tentacles?*"

"Mmmm!" said Darrell, devouring a tentacle. "These are great! Try some, Ben!"

Reluctantly, Ben tried a tentacle. Then he popped a few *bocarones*. Then, with increasing gusto, he tried the chorizo sandwiches and the gazpacho. "Hey, this stuff isn't bad!"

Finally, the paella arrived—a huge mound of saffron yellow rice, suffused with garlic and olive oil and surrounded by generous amounts of sweet red pepper, artichoke hearts, shrimp, chicken, and steaming clams in the shell. "And to think I wanted tacos!" said Ben, helping himself to a liberal serving.

For the next few minutes, the conversation was confined to raves about the food. Then, talk again turned to the subject of the Olympics. "I'm really looking forward to the closing ceremonies," said Judith. "I hear it's going to be as spectacular as that Greek galley they rowed across the field in the opening ceremonies."

"Yeah," said Darrell, "it's a shame Ben has to miss it."

"Oh, really?" said Judith. "Why is that, Ben?"

"Well . . . ," said Ben, uncomfortably.

"Before you got here," Darrell explained, "Ben told me he had some kind of business to take care of, so he was flying back to the States in the morning."

Judith turned to Ben. "What sort of business?" she asked. "Or would that be prying?"

"Personal business," Ben replied, looking away. "Death in the family."

"Oh, I'm sorry, Ben," said Judith.

"Someone close?" asked Darrell.

"No," Ben said hastily. A few moments of silence passed, then, "Well, yes, in a way," he amended lamely. "Actually, it was my dad."

A gasp of surprise escaped Judith's lips and a look of concern crossed her face. "Oh, Ben . . ."

"No big deal, Judith. I haven't talked to my old man in years. Not to put too fine a point on it, the guy was a drunk. And he used to whack me around a lot."

"How did you get the news?" asked Darrell.

"My mom," said Ben. "She tracked me by phone to my hotel room. Called me early this morning and told me all about it. It was a heart attack. Real suddenlike." He sighed deeply. "So. I'm going back for the old man's funeral—not for him but for my mom."

"I thought *something* was bothering you," said Darrell.

"It *doesn't* bother me!" Ben responded, a little too vehemently. "I told you, I haven't seen the guy in years!"

Darrell and Judith just looked at him, saying nothing.

"Hey, guys, don't look at me like that!" said Ben, pumping an extra measure of joviality into his voice. "Don't feel bad on my behalf. I sure don't feel bad. It's not that I hate my old man, or that I'm glad he's dead. Fact is, I never really knew the guy, and it's hard for me to get worked up just because I heard some stranger died." He reached for his shirt pocket where he always kept a pack of Camels. The pocket was empty. "Aw! I smoked the last one in the lobby," he said, standing. "Hey, will you two excuse me for a moment?" he said, getting to his feet, not meeting their eyes. "I've gotta go find a vending machine. I'm all outta coffin nails."

"Sure," said Judith.

"And don't let this thing put a damper on our party, okay?" said Ben, grinning broadly. Too broadly. "This is our last night in Barcelona together. Let's have a good time, okay?"

Judith smiled. "Sure."

"Yeah," said Darrell.

Ben turned and left. Judith watched Ben's unruly thatch of red hair bobbing away through the crowd, then she turned toward Darrell. "I wish he'd just admit that he's hurting inside," she said.

"Yeah," said Darrell. "Did you notice he said the same thing about his 'old man' that he said about God the other night: 'I can take Him or leave Him. No big deal. It doesn't bother me.'"

"You think it *is* a 'big deal,' don't you?"

"All those years of having an abusive father, then a lot more years with no father at all?" Darrell shook his head sadly. "My heart goes out to the guy. I can kind of identify with him."

"Oh?"

"Yeah. I never knew my father. I was raised by my mother, and then she died. It's really rough, not having a father. Not having . . . well, not having something or someone to believe in. You know, I don't think he left just to get a pack of smokes. I think he needed a few minutes to put his happy face back on."

When Ben returned a few minutes later with a pack of Camels in his hand, Judith and Darrell were still talking quietly. He came up behind them and leaned over between them.

"Hey!" Ben shouted. "I just had a great idea!"

"What's that?" asked Judith.

"Where are the ninety-six Summer Olympics going to be held?"

"In Atlanta," said Darrell. "Why?"

Ben clapped his arms around his friends' shoulders. "Wouldn't that be a great place for a reunion?"

"Whose reunion?" asked Judith.

"Ours!" said Ben. "The three of us. You, me, and Darrell. Let's make a pact to get together in Atlanta in ninety-six! What do you say?"

And that's exactly what they did.

PART TWO

The Love of God the Father

CHAPTER SIX

A GENERATION IN SEARCH OF FATHERHOOD

HOW DO WE REACH BEN?

Ben is a fictional character who stands for all the people of our time, both men and women, who have been robbed of the love and security of being parented. Many people in this postmodern age suffer from a distorted conception of God because their earthly parents were abusive, critical, emotionally distant, or absent during their formative years. Others suffer from the corrosive influence of a society that says to them, "Fatherhood is dead. The role of a father must be devalued."

The story Ben longs to hear is a story of a Father's love. That is the aching void in his soul, and in the soul of his entire generation. Ben's generation yearns to experience the truth of the Apostle Paul's closing words to the Corinthians: "May the grace of the Lord Jesus Christ, *and the love of God [the Father]*, and the fellowship of the Holy Spirit be with you all."[1]

What would happen if we were to look at the challenge of evangelism—the challenge of reaching Ben and his generation—

63

through a *new* lens, through a *narrative* lens, the lens of the Story of God? If the story of Ben's life—a story of pain and an absent, unloving earthly father—were to collide with the Story of the love of God the Father, what would happen to Ben? I believe something profound would take place within Ben's heart, within his mind and emotions. I believe the Story of the loving Father would create a Vision in Ben, and that Vision would produce a changed Character within Ben. I believe he would be compelled and moved to join his story (with a small *s*) to the great eternal Story of God.

IN SEARCH OF FATHERHOOD
Did you have a father? Did you know him?

I didn't know my natural father until 1982. I was adopted when I was ten days old. Forty-nine years later, I was sitting in front of my television set, watching Alex Haley's "Roots," and I began to wonder about my own roots. It wasn't that I was driven by a need to know my identity; rather, I wondered if my parents might still be alive and if I could get to know them. After all these years, could I find them? Could I tell them what God has done in my life? Could I thank them for giving me life? The more I thought about it, the more I began to imagine that it was actually possible.

My adoptive parents were both dead by this time. According to Canadian law, if your adoptive parents are deceased, you can apply for a copy of the adoption orders. So, with the help of a friend in Canada where I was born, I began to search for my natural parents. I had a few scraps of information to begin with. I suspected my natural parents had never married, that my mother's father was a clergyman. I knew that the story of my birth was connected with a town in Ontario called Brantford. Using these bits and pieces of information, my Canadian friend, Stan Izon, was able to locate and unseal the documents regarding my adoption.

I was in a hotel in Chicago, not far from O'Hare International Airport, when the documents were first placed in my hands. I examined them eagerly and discovered that the Christian name my birth mother had given me was Peter, and that my mother, who was then sixteen years old, had an Irish last name.

The next step was to contact her. My friend Stan, who was an associate of the Billy Graham Evangelistic Association, located my mother's residence in a town north of Toronto. He called her, identified himself as a member of the Graham organization, and said, "The first thing I want to tell you is that God loves you."

"I know that," she replied. "What else do you want?" She had been hurt and let down many times in her life, and she was justifiably suspicious.

"There is a matter I would like to discuss with you," he replied, "but I'd prefer to discuss it in person rather than on the phone."

Reluctantly, she allowed him to come to her home. On arriving, he explained that he had a friend who was looking for his birth mother. His friend was born in October 1931.

"October twenty-second?" she asked.

"Yes."

She agreed to talk with me. When I called her a week later, I reassured her. "I don't want anything from you. I just want to get to know you, to thank you for giving me life, and to tell you what God has done in my life during the past forty-nine years."

A month later, in September 1980, I drove up to her house. The picture of the first sight of my natural mother is etched forever in my memory. She was wearing a red cardigan, standing in front of her house next to a large pine tree. I got out of the car, walked up to her, gave her a big hug, and said, "My mother." We went inside and talked. She told me she had never forgotten me. Through all these years, she had remembered me every time my birthday came around. Whenever she saw a tall young man walking down the street, she wondered if that could be her son. In fact, she may have heard me preach once in the 1950s—she remembered attending a meeting in a large church at around the same time and place that I had preached early in my career in Canada. We had a long talk and began a relationship that has continued to this day.

Before I left, she told me one other thing: the name of my biological father. With that piece of information as a starting point, it was fairly easy to approach him carefully.

Again, I used an intermediary to establish the connection. It turned out that my father lived in Ontario in the summer and wintered in Sarasota, Florida. So I asked my friend Allan Emery, who lived in Boca Raton, to hand deliver a letter to my father.

Allan decided that the best thing to do in such an unusual situation was to go without any appointment or introduction whatsoever. He drove from the east coast of Florida to the west coast and arrived at my father's home. My father was not there, so Allan waited. Finally, my father pulled up in the driveway. Allan went to the car and introduced himself, then handed my father the very carefully worded letter I had written. Allan waited as he read the letter without comment. Then he said to Allan, "I think I'd better take this inside and think about it."

Allan got to a phone and called me. "Mission accomplished," he said, "but I don't think you'll hear from him."

But about a week later, I did hear from him. My father called and later wrote me and told me about himself. He wanted to meet and talk—but he was not a church-going man and did not want to talk about religion. He also noted the ironic fact that for the past ten years he had driven within five miles of my house every time he traveled between Ontario and his winter home in Florida. I called him, and we agreed to meet near my home in Charlotte. I met him at a shopping center and took him back to our house. He is a tall man, about six-foot-six, with striking white hair and the build of a football tackle. He chain-smoked as we talked.

During our talk, the phone rang. It was Billy Graham. I told Billy that my father was with me, that we had just met and were getting acquainted after all these years, and Billy asked to speak with him. So Billy and my father talked for a few minutes, then my father came back and said to me, "Whew! I just talked to Billy Graham!"

To this day, I continue to keep in touch with my natural father, talking to him several times a year. He is respectful of my religious beliefs, he has been involved with the Sandy Ford Memorial Fund, he has come to hear me speak on several occasions, but he still does not want to discuss spiritual things. (He has reviewed this account, by the way, and has no objection to anything I have said here.)

I identify with a generation that hungers for parenting. Yes, I had loving adoptive parents. They gave me everything a boy could want—except an understanding of my origins, my natural family history. We all long for a sense of our origins, our roots, our meaning, and our place in the world. This is not just an intellectual longing or even an emotional one. In the deepest sense, we all have a *spiritual* longing to know our place in the cosmos, and in eternity. We long to know the God who gave us life—and that we matter to Him.

I now know my natural mother and father. There is a restored relationship that was missing for forty-nine years. That relationship began with a vision in the imagination of my mind and heart. That vision was inspired, you might say, by a story—the story of Alex Haley's "Roots." And the story and the vision that fired my imagination compelled me along a search—a search that brought about a real, tangible relationship.

I see my quest for my natural parents as a metaphor for the quest that so many people of our age—people just like Ben—are engaged in today. Events in their own lives, plus events and social influences in the world around them, are leading many people to ask themselves, "Could it be—is it just barely possible—that there is a God? And that this God is truly a *Father*, and that He cares for me? Could it be that God really is there, and that I matter to Him?" Once this thought occurs, an experiment takes place in the imagination. The heart goes out to God.

This initial wondering phase—the asking of the "Could it be?" question—does not constitute life-changing faith. Rather, it is what the British scholar Austin Farrar has called "initial faith." But it is a *kind* of faith. It is the first tentative groping of a yearning heart in search of a loving heavenly Father. As the writer to the Hebrews says, "Anyone who comes to [God] must believe that he exists and that he rewards those who earnestly seek him."[2] How we seek—whether with an open or closed heart—is vitally important. And today, many people are reexamining the evidence for faith with a new openness.

The Story that there is a God who cares about individual human beings is an old message—but it has been given a new attractiveness, a new plausibility in our time. Our postmodern generation is more ready than ever to hear this Story with new ears. Why? Because of the emptiness and brokenness of postmodern life.

THE DECONSTRUCTION OF FATHERHOOD

The story of Paul de Man is the story of modern man's desire to kill God and the fatherhood that God symbolizes.

Paul de Man was one of the leaders of an influential literary movement called *deconstructionism*. The central tenet of deconstructionism is that words have no objective content, and the effect of deconstructionism is to rob language of its meaning. The term was invented in the 1960s by French philosopher Jacques Derrida, who taught that words are merely subjective constructions with no objective relation to reality. His goal was to "deconstruct" language. In fact, the word *deconstruction* is a combination of the words *destruction* and *construction*. Derrida's goal was to overthrow "logocentrism," the general consensus that *truth* can be assigned to *logos*—to words, to logical reasoning, and specifically to the word (or Word with a capital *W*) of God. Simply put, deconstructionism is an all-out assault on the concept that "words mean things."

Though the deconstructionist movement began as a school of literary criticism, it has since spread to other disciplines. It is, for example, a major force in the radical feminist movement and in most of our country's law schools. Today, our legal profession, our political institutions, and even some theological schools have been infected by this malignant way of thinking. Deconstructionist thought is being used to tear down the meaning of our laws, our social structure, and our religious faith. One of the most profound effects of deconstructionism upon our society and upon our everyday lives is the effect it has had on the way people view matters of faith and spirituality. If words have no meaning, no objective content, then God's Word may be viewed as having no meaning— or it can mean anything we want it to mean.

And whom do we have to thank for the spread of deconstructionism in America? Paul de Man. During the Vietnam era, de Man imported Derrida's ideas to the States and single-handedly established a beachhead for deconstructionist thought at Yale University.

During his tenure there, deconstructionism became a full-fledged academic cult. And from there it quickly spread, cutting a swath across the institutions of our society.

But what kind of man was Paul de Man? In *Signs of the Times: Deconstruction and the Fall of Paul de Man,* David Lehman quotes Hillis Miller, who describes deconstructionists (such as Paul de Man) as a "parricide," a parent-killer, "a bad son demolishing . . . the machine of Western metaphysics."[3] The life of Paul de Man seems to bear out this assessment. Just as the fall of humankind began with the fall of the man Adam, so the fall of our modern world is symbolized in the fall of Paul de Man.

Born in Europe, Paul de Man moved to Buenos Aires where he taught, married, and fathered three children. He abandoned his family and moved to the United States to take a teaching position at Bard College, a small school in New York State. While there he altered his personal history and married one of his students without bothering to divorce his first wife. He was eventually kicked out of Bard College. He left a trail of bad debts, bounced checks, and unpaid landlords in his wake.

Paul de Man's last public lecture at Bard College was a scathing attack on morality, which he considered "destructive." And de Man practiced what he preached, living without regard to any moral codes. He sent no money or messages to the children he left behind, and broke promise after promise to his wife and his ex-wife. Paul de Man scorned his own role as a father, even while he sought to eradicate the Fatherhood of God.

As the ideas of Paul de Man and his fellow deconstructionists have taken root in modern society, the result has been predictable: Society has conformed itself to the deconstructionistic character and image of that Paul de Man symbolizes. Fatherhood in general—and the loving Fatherhood of God in particular—are under vicious assault as part of the culture war in the U.S. In this postmodern era, the role of fatherhood is being eroded, disparaged, and abandoned, with the result that an entire generation is reaching adulthood with a distorted concept of fatherhood and with an unfulfilled longing for parenting. Here is a brief survey of the state of fatherhood in our world today:

Liberal theology dilutes the Fatherhood of God, relegating Him to the role of a sentimental and ineffectual grandfather.

Radical feminism brands God the Father as a patriarchal enemy to be deconstructed and destroyed in an act of patricide. It is tragic and sad that many feminists reject the Fatherhood of God, since Scripture presents God not as a *male* Being, in the human sense, but as a Being with both fatherly and motherly qualities, including the qualities of tenderness and nurturing usually associated with motherhood. The Bible makes it clear that both *men and women* are created in the image of God. As a result of the radical feminists' misunderstanding of the inclusive nature of the gospel and the tender, nurturing character of God, many of them have turned to the practice of "sheology," the worship of a goddess rather than God. They have attempted to reinvent God in their own image instead of worshiping the God in whose image they themselves were lovingly created.

As Judith Weinraub wrote in the *Washington Post*, radical feminists "are looking for a spiritual connection—for a way to push the boundaries of their religious experience beyond the ordinary confines of traditional Judeo-Christian monotheism. . . . Not for them the patriarchal structure of the male-dominated religions of the Old and New Testaments. Their touchstones are the pagan religions, the pre-Christian Earth-centered goddess cults that stress the harmony of the universe—movements that offer equality rather than hierarchy, peace rather than war, joy rather than guilt, ritual rather than rote." The goal of these goddess worshipers is to redefine God in nonmasculine, nonfatherly terms.

As an example, Weinraub cites the story of Susan, a Philadelphia mother and self-described "radical feminist witch not yet out of the broom closet." Susan was raised in a deeply religious Presbyterian home, but was alienated by "the anti-sexuality, anti-sensuality, the guilt and sin and punishment rather than joy. From the time I was a little kid, I couldn't accept redemptive suffering. Why is the central metaphor of most religions the bloody violent death of a male? Why is it not birth?" Tragically, this woman has rejected the Story that is the ultimate expression of a Father's love, and she has chosen instead to join her story to a pagan goddess myth.[4]

Much of *modern psychology* treats the Fatherhood of God as a myth to be explained away. This "explanation" for the "God-myth" can be traced back to Ludwig Feuerbach (1804–1872), the German materialist philosopher and student of Hegel. Feuerbach was a great influence on Karl Marx, and Feuerbach's ideas largely fueled the relentless godlessness of the Communist system—a system that spent seventy years in an attempt to exterminate God the Father.

Faith in God, said Feuerbach, owes its existence to the needy, battered condition of our human psyche. We invent God as a cosmic "daddy" to comfort us. In other words, he's saying God didn't create us in His image; we created Him in ours. According to Feuerbach's "projection theory" of religion, God is merely a projection of our subconscious psychological needs. Just as a slide projector enlarges a tiny image from a piece of film and projects it onto a wide screen, so we project a fantasy we call "God the Father" onto a cosmic screen, the universe itself. This fantasy, he says, is nothing more than an enlarged image of our own puny selves. Despite the collapse of Communism, Feuerbach's ideas continue to affect our world through such fields as psychology, psychiatry, philosophy, and the arts. Because of these ideas, many people have concluded (with a certain degree of smugness), "Now that I know God is just a psychological projection, I don't need the crutch of the God-myth in my life. I have no need of a 'heavenly Father.'"

Islam, the great global competitor to Christianity, presents God—Allah—as the Great, the Beneficent, the Ruler. But for Muslims, Allah is not a Father. In fact, to the Muslim, associating omnipotent Allah with human beings or human characteristics is the sin of *shirk*, the greatest sin. So the Muslims do not speak of a loving heavenly Father.

We can see the terrible effect of fatherlessness in the life of one particular Muslim, the strongman-leader of Iraq, Saddam Hussein. By the standards of Iraqi culture, Saddam Hussein is a "fatherless" man, born under very unusual circumstances. His father had divorced his mother, and later wanted to marry her again, but due to a quirk in the law, he couldn't remarry her until there had been a death or a divorce. So Saddam's father arranged for another man to enter into a marriage of convenience with his ex-wife, a marriage in which there was to be no sexual intercourse. The second husband would then divorce Saddam's mother so that his father could be legally married. But Saddam Hussein was conceived in that interim marriage, and was always looked upon by his half-dozen brothers and sisters as a bastard child. He was sent off to his uncle when he was seven, and his uncle introduced him to Ba'ath politics.

It is probable that much of the cruelty and violence of Saddam's character are the result of the pain and anger stored up in the life of a rejected little boy who knew no earthly father and no heavenly Father. That childhood pain and anger were later magnified into bloodshed and warfare when the wounded boy became a political strongman.

This is not to say that Saddam's story is typical of all young boys growing up in the Muslim culture. Many Muslim boys have strong, caring, available fathers. But in countries such as Iraq and Iran, where so many fathers have died in so-called holy wars, there are thousands of young boys growing up fatherless—without knowing an earthly father or a heavenly Father. And it's sobering to think of all the pain and anger they are storing up right now to unleash on the world of the future—along with the rage that is accumulating in the hearts of fatherless boys even in this country.

Secular materialism views God the Father as an outmoded relic of the past. Secular people see the Christian faith as old-fashioned and irrelevant. Most secular people today are not outright atheists; rather, many are *deists*. Like the eighteenth-century natural philosopher John Locke, they believe in God, though not a loving, personal God. Rather, they believe that God is a cosmic watchmaker. He constructed the universe like a great watch, wound it up and set it running, then walked away. Now the universe is running down. "Yes, there's a God, a Power, a Force out there," they say, "but God couldn't be interested in me and my problems. How could He be? In this wide universe of ours, with its billions of galaxies, and with billions of stars in each galaxy, how could God possibly care for an individual human being like me?"

Secular people have been schooled to believe that God—if

there is a God—is too removed, too remote to care about a single individual. They need to hear the good news that not even a sparrow can fall without the Father's concern, and that God knows all human beings so well that the very hairs on their heads are numbered. They need to hear that God is not only *infinite*, He is also *intimate*. He is a personal, fatherly God. Where secular people are encountering God today, it is usually not because they have been rationally convinced by a mountain of empirical evidence. Rather, it is because they have encountered a Father who cares.

Someone once asked Leith Anderson, a pastor in Minnesota, "If you had just one sentence to say to secular people, what would you say?" His reply: "I'd say, 'You matter to God.'" That's what most secular people don't know: God made them and God loves them. And people today—whether empty Marxists, searching Muslims, angry radicals, or secular materialists—are longing, whether they consciously know it or not, to hear our Story, a Story that says, "God made you, and you matter to God."

CHAPTER SEVEN

An Old Story for a New Age

OUR STORY: THE LOVE OF GOD THE FATHER

There is a story—probably apocryphal but certainly full of meaning and truth—about a Roman emperor who was returning victorious from a battlefield. He was standing in his chariot, leading a parade of soldiers through the streets of Rome. On every side, crowds were cheering his return.

As the chariot passed, a young boy broke through the line of guards who were restraining the crowd along the road. One of the guards tried to catch the boy, but the boy wriggled out of his grasp and ran straight for the chariot. "Stop!" the guard commanded. "No one may approach the emperor!"

But the boy just laughed and called back, "He may be *your* emperor, but he's *my* father!" And the boy leaped aboard the moving chariot and was lifted and embraced by his father, the emperor of Rome.

As we look at the task of evangelism through a narrative lens, the lens of the Story of God, we see that we have a lot to say to this postmodern generation, especially through the Story of the love of God the Father. Even though the concept of fatherhood has become battered and bruised in our society, and even though this generation thinks it has lost hope of ever finding a loving Father, there is a deep yearning for *parenting* in the people around us. You and I know what it means to have a heavenly Father, a Parent who loves us, who forgives, who lifts us when we fall, who draws us into an intimate relationship with Him. That Story and that vision should so transform our character that we can't keep from telling others the Story of a Father who loves them too.

AN EVANGELISM FOR OUR TIMES

Walter Fisher, professor of communication arts and sciences at the University of Southern California, has suggested a new paradigm that may help us bridge the gulf between the modern, rational, *logos*-oriented mind and the postmodern, deconstructionist mind. He has observed that the modern world operates under certain assumptions, which he grouped together and labeled *the rational paradigm*. The assumptions of the rational paradigm include:

- The belief that people are essentially rational and logical.
- The belief that people make decisions on the basis of rational arguments and logical evidence.
- The belief that the world is a set of logical puzzles to be solved through rational analysis.

Deconstructionism—being an anti-*logos*, anti-rational way of thinking—seeks to abolish the rational paradigm. Fisher proposes that a new paradigm—which he calls *the narrative paradigm*—is better suited to the way people really think than the rational paradigm. The assumptions of the narrative paradigm include:

- The belief that people are essentially storytellers.
- The belief that people make decisions on the basis of stories that are coherent and that "ring true" when tested against reality.

■ The belief that the world is a set of stories we use to shape our view of ourselves and our reality.

This means that *narrative evangelism is an evangelism for the times we live in*—a postmodern, anti-rational, deconstructed age. This does not mean that a rational evangelism is invalid. Evangelism that is rooted in the logical nature of the gospel, the verifiable claims of Christ, and the clear evidence of the Resurrection has always been valid and effective. But rational arguments are not as persuasive in our postmodern age as they were in the modern era. A new evangelism, based on a narrative paradigm, is the evangelism of the postmodern era. It presents the Story that rings true when tested against reality, and it meets the need of people who are looking for a story with which to shape their view of themselves and their view of reality.

A Christian, says J. I. Packer, is a person "who has God as Father." That is the Story we have to tell to Ben and the rest of his fatherless generation. "You sum up the whole of the New Testament teaching in a single phrase," Packer adds, "if you speak of it as a revelation of the Fatherhood of the holy Creator." And the one characteristic that, more than any other, truly defines the Fatherhood of God is the characteristic of *love*. As 1 John 3:1 tells us, "How great is the love the Father has lavished on us, that we should be called children of God!"

The Bible gives us a Story that is unerringly targeted on the hearts of postmodern men and women. This Story can be simply summarized:

■ God made the members of the human race and placed them in His world to make it a place of beauty.
■ God bound Himself to be their God.
■ God assigned them special duties.
■ When they turned away from Him, God judged them.
■ But God also made a decision to rescue them from judgment.
■ He sent His Son to tell them that He loves them and wants them to come home.

The Bible is rich in imagery that vividly describes the Fatherhood of God. In the Old Testament, God is presented as the Father-Creator of the entire human race. "Have we not all one Father?" says Malachi 2:10. "Did not one God create us?" And the Old Testament also presents God as the Father of the nation of Israel. "This is what the LORD says: Israel is my firstborn son," says God in Exodus 4:22.

But the New Testament reveals an even deeper dimension of God's Fatherhood, portraying Him as an *intimate, personal* Father— not of all people but specifically of those who put their trust in His Son, Jesus Christ, as their sin-bearer. "You are all sons of God," says the Apostle Paul in Galatians 3:26, "through faith in Christ Jesus." This intimate relationship with God the Father is not a universal status conferred on all people by natural birth. Rather, it is a supernatural gift that comes through receiving Jesus as Lord and Savior—the second birth.

It is not a natural sonship but an adoptive sonship. "You received the Spirit of sonship," says Romans 8:15. "And by him we cry, '*Abba,* Father.'" That word *Abba* is an Aramaic term best translated "Daddy," the sound a trusting little child would make while being lifted into the strong arms of his or her loving father. So while the Old Testament presented only the holiness and omnipotence of God, the New Testament has introduced us to the *intimate* dimension of God, presenting Him as our *Abba,* our adopted Daddy, the loving Parent we all yearn to know. And this is the good news that Ben and his generation are longing to hear: As children of this loving Father, we have been given the right to draw near to Him, in boldness and in trust.

In the deep heart of the world, I am convinced, there is a longing to hear the Story of an accessible, approachable, loving God. Imagine how this world would be transformed if you and I and every other person who knows this Story would take it, live it, and tell it to the disillusioned Marxists and Muslims who have never known a heavenly Father; to the empty secular materialists who are desperately trying to fill their Father-shaped void with things that cannot satisfy; to people like Ben, adult children of absent fathers and dysfunctional fathers. Imagine the transformation in individual lives and in an entire society that this Story could bring!

OUR VISION: SEEING PEOPLE AS GOD SEES THEM

Bilquis Sheikh is a former Muslim who was brought to faith in Christ by the Story of the love of God the Father. Looking back on his spiritual pilgrimage, he describes the moment when the Story seized his imagination and produced a vision in his life:

> A breakthrough of hope flooded me. Suppose God were like a father? If my earthly father would put aside everything to listen to me, wouldn't my heavenly Father do the same? Shaking with excitement, I got out of bed, sank to my knees on the rug, looked up to heaven, and in a rich new understanding called God "My Father." I wasn't prepared for what happened. Hesitantly, I spoke His name aloud: "Father. Father God." I tried different ways of speaking to Him. And then as if something broke through for me, I found myself trusting that He was hearing me, as my earthly father had done. "I'm confused, Father," I said. "I have to get one thing straight right away."
>
> I reached over to the bedside table where I kept the Bible and the Koran side by side. I picked up both books and lifted them, one in each hand. "Which, Father? Which one is Your Book?" And then a remarkable thing happened. Nothing like it has ever occurred in my life in quite this way. I heard a voice inside my being, a voice . . . full of kindness, yet at the same time full of authority. And the voice said, "In which book do you meet Me as your Father?" I found myself answering, "In the Bible." That's all it took.[1]

The Story became a vision in the life of a Muslim named Bilquis Sheikh—and that vision transformed his life. Now the question that confronts you and me is: What is *our* vision? What motivates us and moves us toward people like Ben, toward people like Bilquis Sheikh? What motivates us to reach out and share the Story of the love of the Father with that neighbor or classmate or coworker we see and talk to every day? What motivates us to evangelize?

I would suggest to you that the purest motivation for evangelism of all is *vision*. And when I say "vision," I don't mean it in the sense it is so often used today—a plan, a strategy, or an entrepreneurial program. In the sense I use it here, *vision* means to see the world, and all the people in it, as God the Father sees them. And there is no better way to catch God's vision for lost people and a lost world than to begin with a story—the story that Jesus Himself told.

We encounter that story in Luke 15. In fact we encounter three stories in that chapter, and all three have a common theme: something extremely valuable is lost; a search takes place at great cost; and great rejoicing ensues when that which was lost is finally found. These three stories—the story of the lost sheep, the story of the lost coin, and the story of a lost son and his loving father—all speak of our immense value to God, how He searches for us, and how He rejoices over us when we are found.

The capstone of the Luke 15 trilogy is the third parable, "The Story of the Loving Father" (usually mistitled "The Story of the Prodigal Son"). The story is familiar to all Christians: an ungrateful, self-centered son demands and receives his inheritance from his father. The son goes away, spends everything he has on wild hedonistic living, then returns home in disgrace. To his amazement, he is lovingly, exuberantly received by his father—though he is resented by his older brother. It has been called the most beautiful story ever told, but we usually miss the point of it. We mistell this story in three ways:

1. We tell it to the wrong audience, to the prodigals in the rescue mission. Yes, they need to hear it, too, but I don't think they are the primary audience Jesus intended for this story. Jesus gave this story, remember, to the religious leaders. The audience Jesus primarily intended for this story was not an audience of prodigals but an audience of "religious" people, "church" people—maybe people like you and me.
2. We give this story the *wrong title*—"The Prodigal Son." In fact, this is the story of two sons (the prodigal and his older brother), their father, and this father's amazing love.

3. Most important of all, we hear this story with *wrong ears,*
   with Western cultural ears, and thus we miss the profound
   shock value of this story.

To understand the point Jesus was making with this story, we need
to put ourselves into the cultural and social context in which it was
told. Look with me at the opening verses of the chapter: "Now the
tax collectors and 'sinners' were all gathering around to hear [Jesus].
But the Pharisees and the teachers of the law muttered, 'This man
welcomes sinners and eats with them.'"[2] The religious leaders
were complaining and opposing Jesus because He was not
respectable, and did not keep respectable company! He welcomed
sinners! He even ate with them!

In response, Jesus told three stories about lost things. His point
was that these religious leaders didn't know what sin really is.
They thought of sin as *badness.* But in these stories, Jesus demonstrated that sin is actually *awayness.* The sheep, the coin, and the
son were all *away* from those who treasured them. The sheep were
away from the shepherd, the coin was away from the woman who
prized it, the son was away from the father and his home. All of
these objects had one thing in common: they were missing. Only
when they were found and the relationship was restored could joy
be complete.

Kenneth Bailey, who spent many years teaching at the Near
East School of Theology in Beirut, has written an insightful study
of this parable called *The Cross and the Prodigal.* In that book,
Bailey helps us to see the story through the eyes of Middle Eastern
villagers. He did this by actually going from village to village in the
Middle East and telling this parable to people, then asking, "What
is your reaction to this story?" Like the villagers and religious leaders who gathered around Jesus in Luke 15, most of these Middle
Eastern people were hearing this story for the first time. After
telling it, Bailey would then ask, "Have you ever heard of anything like that happening in your village?" The unanimous reply:
"Never!"

Next question: "Well, what would happen if a son came to his
father and said, 'Give me my inheritance'?" Reply: "Why, the

father would beat him on his head! He's saying to his father, 'Drop dead! I can't wait for you to die, old man! Get out of my way!'"

"And what would happen if the boy came back home, penniless, hungry, and broken?" The Middle Eastern reply: "The father would certainly not run to him and receive him! The father would stay hidden for a while and make the son eat humble pie outside the gate of the village. The children would recognize him and mock him. He would be shamed and humiliated for what he did."

But that's not what happens in Jesus' story. The father in Luke 15 does what no other Middle Eastern father would do: He *runs* to his son, forgetting his dignity, forgetting the insult and disrespect his son had shown him. He doesn't care about any of that. He only wants to have his son home again. He wraps the boy in his arms and says, "My son was dead and is alive again! Let's throw a party for him!"

Our vision for evangelism emerges as we identify with the father in that story, as we look out across our neighborhoods and our world and see the shame and the misery of all those prodigal people. We receive our vision as we look at the world through the loving eyes of the Father. That is the vision that must grip our imagination as we look into the eyes of the people around us at the office, on the campus, and over the back fence. That is the vision that transforms our character, that changes us so that we become natural storytellers, living and sharing the Story of God's love.

OUR MOTIVE FOR WITNESSING:
THE JOY OF THE FATHER

One of the plot threads of the film *Chariots of Fire* concerns the story of Eric Liddell, a Scottish runner in the 1924 Olympics who later served and died as a missionary to China. In the film, Eric's Olympic aspirations are opposed by his devoutly Christian sister, Jenny, who fears that the fame and acclaim of Olympic competition will go to Eric's head and turn him away from his missionary calling. His sister's fears create a deep emotional conflict for Eric, which is finally resolved in a scene where Eric takes Jenny up on a hillside and tells her of the decision he has made. "I've decided," he tells her. "I'm going back to China. The missionary service has accepted me."

Thrilled, Jenny hugs him. "I'm so pleased!" she says.

But Liddell isn't finished. "I'm going to China, Jenny," he says, "but I've got a lot of running to do first. I must compete in the Olympic Games. You've got to understand. I believe God made me for a purpose, for China. But He also made me *fast*. And when I run, I feel His *pleasure*."

Eric Liddell had found the best motive for doing anything in life, whether it be running in the Olympics or taking the Story of God halfway around the world: Liddell chose to do whatever would give *pleasure* to God.

Why do we evangelize? Because we have a Great Commission from our Lord? Absolutely—and we must obey it. Because people are lost? Yes, the god of this world has blinded the minds of those who are lost forever, apart from Jesus Christ. Because people have needs and hurts? Yes, more than we can imagine.

But the great thought that ought to seize our hearts and fill us with an overpowering, compelling vision is this truth, embedded in the Story of the loving Father: When the lost are found, it gives *joy* to God—joy beyond our ability to comprehend. At the close of every day, we should stop to take stock of our vision for evangelism. We should ask ourselves, "Is there anything in my life this day that has opened a door for a prodigal daughter or prodigal son to come back home? Is there anything I have done today to bring joy and pleasure to the Father's heart?"

Some years ago, Billy Graham was preaching at Angels Stadium in California. It was a tremendous crusade—especially so in view of all the ethnic groups represented. In fact, the middle tier of Angels Stadium was divided into sections, each of which was equipped with earphones so that people could hear the gospel in their own language. One section had a banner reading "Vietnamese," another "Hispanics," another "Korean," another "Hindi," and on and on.

I was there the first night Billy gave the invitation. I remember seeing people streaming out of their seats and moving across the stadium. If you've seen Billy Graham on television, you know how he stands during the invitation with his head bowed and his chin in his hands, praying. During this particular invitation, something happened that surprised Billy Graham. While the choir was singing "Just As I Am," people began applauding. At that moment, I saw Billy's head raise up in surprise. I knew what he was thinking, because I was thinking the very same thing: *What is happening here? No one ever applauds during the invitation!*

Billy turned to the crowd and said, "Please be quiet. This is not the time for applause." But the people kept clapping!

And then we found out why. Ten Vietnamese people had gotten up from their section and were coming forward to receive Christ—and other Vietnamese Christians were applauding them! They were filled with joy—the same kind of joy that filled the heart of the prodigal's father when he saw his boy coming home! These Vietnamese Christians were saying, "Our people are coming to Jesus!" Well, this spirit of joy just caught on and spread throughout that middle tier of the stadium. Soon the Laotians were cheering their people who were coming to Jesus. And the Pakistanis. And the Hispanics. And the Koreans. Section after section after section.

I saw this realization dawn on Billy's face. Then he stepped up to the microphone again and said, "You know, it does say in the Bible that there is joy among the angels in the presence of God over one sinner who repents—and after all, we are in Angels Stadium! So I guess it's okay if you applaud!"

It gives God pleasure whenever people join their stories to God's Story, and our pleasure is to do whatever gladdens the heart of God. That is the vision that produces the character of an evangelist within each of us. When we look at the world and the people around us through the narrative lens of Luke 15, when we catch a glimpse of the heart of the Father, as modeled by the prodigal's father, we can't help but be transformed. Our character will be transformed, and our witness will be transformed.

OUR CHARACTER: THE FATHER'S
LOVE MODELED IN OUR LIVES

How is our *character* changed by the expanded vision we have of a loving Father? And how does our transformed character attract people to the Story of God? Answer: Our character is displayed in our actions, and through our actions, people see God.

Jim Petersen, who worked with The Navigators in Brazil, tried for a long time to reach a Communist student for Christ. This student was a tough case. Jim taught him, befriended him, and debated spiritual issues with him for months. Finally, this student gave his life to the Lord. Jim later asked him, "What did I say that reached you?"

"Nothing," the student replied.

"Nothing!" Jim was dumbfounded.

"Oh, I listened," the student went on. "I was searching and questioning, and you answered a lot of my intellectual questions. But it wasn't what you *said* that changed my heart. It was what you *did*."

Now Jim was *really* baffled. "What did I do?" he asked.

"Nothing spectacular," the student replied. "It's just that you were a friend to me. You invited me into your home. And that's how I got to find out what kind of guy you really are. Jim, I watched the way you disciplined your children—with grace and toughness, and above all with love. *And I saw God in the way you lived with your children.*"

This young student was evangelized through the character of Jim Petersen. He saw the love of God the Father being lived out in the story of Jim's life. That is the most convincing story of all—the Story of God as it is written upon a human life.

In the Sermon on the Mount, Jesus taught that our character is our greatest witness to the Father, and that our daily conduct is to be a glowing testimony to His love. By our lives, we are to bring praise to God and make Him proud of us. "Let your light shine before men," said Jesus, "that they may see your good deeds and praise your Father in heaven."[3] Jesus went on to say that we are to imitate our Father and to show the family likeness of the Father. How do we do this? By showing His unique brand of *love* to the people around us. "You have heard that it was said, 'Love your neighbor and hate your enemy,'" said Jesus. "But I tell you: Love your enemies and pray for those who persecute you, that you may be sons of your Father in heaven."[4] In those words, Jesus introduced a kind of love that the world had never heard of before, and still can scarcely understand.

When we speak of love in our culture, we may mean *eros*

love—the love of beauty, passionate love, romantic love, sexual love. Or we might mean *storge* love—family love. Or we might mean *phileo* love—the love of friendship for those who are near and dear to us. But when God loves, He loves with *agape* love—love that is not rooted in emotion but in the will. *Agape* love is a decision and a commitment to the highest good of the person being loved. *Agape* love is the only kind of love that can carry out the command of Christ to love our enemies, to love those who hurt us and wish us harm. All forms of love have some emotional component; but *agape* love is a choice we can make with our will, a choice that goes beyond our emotions. *Agape* love is like the rudder that guides the ship steadily, despite shifting weather patterns. When we love with *agape* love, we are imitating the love and the character of God the Father—and, says Jesus, when we love with *agape* love, we mark ourselves as children of the heavenly Father.

Jesus goes on to say that our prayer life is nothing more or less than having a conversation with a loving Father. We can trust Him to meet all our needs. "Your Father knows what you need before you ask him," says Jesus. "Look at the birds of the air; they do not sow or reap or store away in barns, and yet your heavenly Father feeds them. Are you not much more valuable than they?"[5] When the people around us see our transformed character, when they see the way we love others with the Father's unique brand of unconditional *agape* love, when they see the trusting way we pray and live out our lives, then they will see God's Story written in our lives. Evangelism in a postmodern age must take on the character not only of *speaking* the truth, but of *modeling* the truth on a daily basis. People will know what kind of Father we have as they see what kind of fathers and mothers *we* are, what kind of husbands and wives *we* are, what kind of supervisors and employers *we* are, what kind of teachers and mentors *we* are. Mere words are not enough to convince men and women like Ben. They must see the love of God the Father in action. They must see the vibrant, dynamic *character* of God's people. They must see real integrity and consistency in Christians. They must see faithful covenant love in fathers and families and churches.

When our love is like God's own unconditional *agape* love,

people can't help but be challenged, because the Father's love is completely unlike the love of this world. When our generation comes face-to-face with the character of God's people, the story of their lives will collide head-on with the Story of God. Their own stories will be called into question. They will be forced to reexamine their lives, their values, and the foundations of their beliefs. And many will be convinced, and will make a decision to merge their stories with the Greatest Story Ever Told.

WHAT IF ... ?
Ben's father was a alcoholic, an abuser, and an absent stranger throughout most of Ben's life. But what if Ben were to somehow discover the love of God the Father? What if a Christian were to come into Ben's life and model the love of the Father in a tangible way? How might Ben's life be changed?

CHAPTER EIGHT

STORY:
Reunion in Atlanta

THE SUMMER OLYMPICS: JULY 1996

Even though Darrell had to park his '96 Camaro four blocks from the restaurant, he still managed to arrive a few minutes early. He strolled up Piedmont until he caught sight of the familiar polished-steel and neon facade of The Buckhead Diner. He hoped Ben and Judith would have no problem getting there. Trying to find a cab in this town during the Olympics could be murder.

He pushed through the big glass door of the restaurant and was instantly overwhelmed with the sights, sounds, and aromas of his favorite eating establishment. The place had the feel of a dining car on the Orient Express, only many times more spacious. It was adorned with a black-and-white marble floor; trainlike transom windows; a big neon, stainless-steel clock; and rich woods everywhere—mahogany, ebony, and maple. As Darrell knew it would be, the restaurant (one of Atlanta's trendiest) was wall-to-wall people—mostly Generation X-ers like himself—and it was raucous with friendly babble, laughter, and the clink of silverware on fine Dudsen china.

Darrell inspected the crowd that jammed the vestibule, seach-
ing for a path to the hostess stand—then he saw what he was *really*
looking for: a shock of unruly red hair standing out above the heads
of the crowd. Like a heat-seeking missile, Darrell aimed for that
patch of auburn and soon found himself within a few feet of Ben's
back, blocked only by a couple who were arguing over whose fault
it was that they were late and would have to wait ninety minutes
for a table. "Excuse me," said Darrell, reaching between them to
tap the red-haired man on the shoulder.

The man turned, and for a brief instant Darrell thought it was
a case of mistaken identity; unlike the Ben he remembered, *this*
red-haired man also had a beard. But then he realized that the face
behind the beard was indeed Ben's.

"Darrell!" called Ben, his eyes wide and his voice carrying
well above the din of the crowd.

"Ben!" Darrell replied, moving around the arguing couple to
get within reach of his old friend. Darrell thrust out his hand and
Ben grabbed it and pumped it in a powerful two-fisted grip.

"It's great to see you, man!" shouted Ben. "I didn't think you'd
recognize me! How did you see through my disguise?"

"That beard?" asked Darrell, laughing. "You call *that* a disguise? Ben, those flaming auburn chin whiskers are as conspicu-
ous as your flaming auburn locks! You stand out in a crowd now
more than you ever did!"

"You're looking good, Darrell!"

"You, too, man! How long have you been waiting?"

"Oh, I've been here since—"

"Darrell! Ben!"

The two men turned. It was Judith. Her hair was short with
feathered bangs, and despite the sultry weather of Atlanta in July,
she looked cool in a peach-colored Parisian tunic, vest, and wide-
leg pants.

"Judith!" Ben and Darrell said in unison.

Judith pushed through the crowd and gave them each a hug.
"Isn't this great!" she said. "Together again in Atlanta!"

Then their hostess arrived to guide them to their table. When
they were shown to a table in the nonsmoking section, Judith

nodded in Ben's direction and said, "Excuse me, our friend needs a table in the smoking section."

The hostess turned to Ben and said, "I'm sorry, I thought you said—"

"I did," Ben replied. "Nonsmoking. This table will be fine, thanks." Then to Judith he added, "I don't smoke those things anymore."

Darrell was amazed. "The human chimney has given up smoking? I don't believe it!"

"Yep. I gave ol' Joe Camel the heave-ho about eighteen months ago."

"I guess we've all been through some big changes in the past four years," said Judith.

"Well, let's sit down and talk about it," said Darrell. "We've got a lot of catching up to do."

They seated themselves and ordered drinks, then Judith opened her purse. "Look," she said, grinning. Tilting the purse open, she spilled out about a dozen pamphlets. "Remember how mad I was at those Christian pamphleteers in Barcelona. Well, they followed me all the way to Atlanta. I swear, some of the same street preachers that were hassling me on the Ramblas are out there in Lennox Square!"

"Then why are you smiling?" asked Darrell. "Four years ago, those people made you go ballistic!"

"Let's just say," Judith replied cryptically, "that I understand those people a little better than I used to."

Darrell was about to ask her what she meant, but the waiter chose that moment to take their orders. While they waited for dinner to arrive, they talked about the spectacular opening ceremonies, and speculated on who would take home the gold in various events. It was only the first day, so the entire XXVI Olympiad lay ahead of them, full of excitement and expectation. Soon, dinner arrived and the conversation continued over a repast of smoked salmon tostadas with papaya salsa, Delmonico steak, mostaccioli with sausage and Asiago, and jalapeño coleslaw.

"Mmm! The food is fabulous!" declared Judith. "You really do know your restaurants, Darrell."

"Yeah," Ben marveled. "When you said we'd meet at a 'diner,' I pictured some kind of greasy spoon, but *this* place—Wow!"

"Well, wining and dining around Atlanta is a big part of my job," said Darrell, grinning.

"Speaking of jobs," said Judith, "Ben, I just couldn't believe it when I got your note and it was postmarked Oshkosh, Wisconsin! Oshkosh, b'gosh! Whatever happened to your dream of coming to New York and writing for *Sports Illustrated?*"

"Well, Judith," Ben said with a grin, "life has a way of taking unexpected turns. I must have made a hundred phone calls and written five hundred letters, but nothing ever opened up at *SI*. Well, I was getting tired of beating my head against that particular wall, and I was getting tired of Chicago. A friend told me about a position opening up at the *Daily Northwestern* in Oshkosh, so I applied and I got the job as sports editor. I've never been sorry. In fact, that move was the best thing that ever happened to me."

"How so?" asked Darrell.

Ben leaned back and sighed. "Where do I begin? First off, I'm a different person than I was four years ago. And I mean, *really* different. It started when I moved to Oshkosh. I hadn't really made any friends yet, and I was down at the racquet club, knocking a handball around by myself. While I was there, this guy introduced himself and asked me to join him in a game. His name was Don, and he was a tough competitor on the court—yet really easy to talk to off the court. Don and his wife, Salli, had me over for dinner a few times and they befriended me, took me under their wing. After I had known Don for about a month, he invited me to his house to. . . . Well, how do I put this?"

"He invited you over to do what?" prompted Darrell.

"To study the Bible."

"*What?!*" said Judith in surprise. "My old agnostic buddy Ben? In a *Bible* study?"

"I know, I know, that's exactly what I thought! 'Me? In a Bible study?' Crazy, right? Well, I told Don I didn't know the first thing about the Bible. But he said, 'That's okay, most of the people in our group are at the same place you are. No one's expected to have all the answers. In fact, there are no right or wrong answers—just a group of people trying to apply the Bible to their own lives.'

"So I went—just to see what it was like. Well, I was really surprised. In fact, I liked it! And I kept coming back. As I listened to other people talking about the Bible and about their own lives, I realized I had some questions of my own: How do we know Jesus really lived? Can a modern, educated person really believe the Bible? Can we actually know God as a Father, like Jesus said? This was all new to me.

"But what really got to me was Don himself. He talked openly in the group about his own life. Turns out he and I have a lot in common. His dad was a salesman, so was mine. His dad was an alcoholic, so was mine. There was abuse in his family, just like mine. Of course, there were differences, too. Don was able to reconcile with his dad, and my dad died while he was still a stranger to me. But the important thing I learned from Don was that I can start over with a *brand-new* father."

"What do you mean," asked Darrell, " a 'brand-new father'?"

"Well, it's kind of a long story," said Ben. "But maybe I can condense it to just a few events from these past couple years. Around the same time I joined Don's group, I ran into a series of problems. First, I got really sick. Some kinda combination of mononucleosis and strep, the doctor said. I was down for the count, weak as a baby—and these people from Don's group became like a family to me, bringing me meals, running errands for me, driving me to the doctor.

"Then, just as I was getting over the bug and getting back to work, my house was broken into. The burglars cleaned out everything of value, then set fire to the place to try to cover it up. The fire was contained in one room, but there was smoke and water damage all over the place. It was a real mess, and the insurance company only wanted to give me a third of what it was worth. I wasn't thinking too clearly, and I was ready to settle, but then Don stepped in and guided me through the process. Don's in the insurance business, and even though he wasn't my agent, he gave hours of his time to help me get a fair settlement. On top of that, people from the group helped me with the cleaning and repainting so the place could be livable again.

"Finally, Don went with me to Smokers Anonymous, and helped me kick my addiction to the weed. He's a former Camels addict himself. Until I met Don, I was resigned to the fact that cigarettes were going to kill me—but he helped me beat 'em.

"I had known Don for about six months or so, and I finally asked him, 'Why are you doing this? I can never repay you for everything you and Salli and others in the Bible study group have done in my life.' He said, 'Ben, you don't owe me anything. Fact is, if I can help you out in any way, that's just a small payment on the debt I owe to God the Father. You have no idea how many times His people have helped me over the years. The best thing about a debt like that is that you just keep it in circulation. Somebody helps me, I help you, you help the next guy, and God gets all the credit, because it was His idea all along.'

"I just couldn't believe it—all this acceptance and help for me, for somebody Don just met on the handball court. Don and these other people became my *family*—not like the dysfunctional family I came from, but a *real* family where people care for you and the communication lines are wide open and people are honest and caring and help you to become a better person. And it was in that group that I found out that I have a real Father—" Ben's voice faltered and choked, and his eyes puddled up.

Judith was thunderstruck. When they were in journalism school together, Ben was always "Good-Time Charlie," a perennial joker, always keeping his real self buried, keeping conversations superficial, instantly deflecting any discussion of feelings. Seeing real emotion on Ben's face, Judith thought, *This man has really changed!*

Ben dabbed at his eyes and brought his voice under control. "I mean, I finally have a Father who loves me. Instead of kicking me when I fall down, He picks me up and puts me on my feet again. Instead of telling me how stupid I am or how ashamed He is of me, this Father says, 'Try again, you can do it.' The Father I'm talking about is *God* the Father. I'm . . . I'm a Christian now. So there you have it, guys. Your old agnostic buddy Ben has become one of those religious fanatics. Fact is—and you're really not going to believe this—I'm a deacon in the church!"

All around the restaurant, there was the babble of conversation and the clatter of dinnerware. But at the table of Ben, Judith, and Darrell, there was only stunned silence.

Finally, Ben broke the silence. Looking from Darrell to Judith and back to Darrell again, he said, "You guys are staring at me like I've got two heads!"

The silence around the table dissolved into gales of laughter. Yet Ben's surprise announcement that he was now a Christian was just the first of *several* surpises of the evening. . . .

PART THREE

The Grace of the Son

CHAPTER NINE

THE STORY MADE VISIBLE

HOW DO WE REACH JUDITH?

Our fatherless, agnostic friend Ben has found faith in Christ because someone took the time to befriend him and introduce him to the love of God the Father. Ben's friend Don not only *talked* about the gospel Story, but he *lived* the Story in such a way that Ben found it irresistible. It was a Story that was exactly the right shape and size to fit the void in Ben's life—a void where the presence of a father's love was supposed to be.

Now we turn to Ben's friend Judith. How will we reach her?

Judith is a liberal, Jewish television producer for a major network—keen, perceptive, ambitious, and secularized in her values, her lifestyle, and her worldview. When we met her in Barcelona, we saw that Judith is deeply concerned about world peace and the environment, and she has been investigating New Age beliefs, including the goddess religion. She is strongly biased against traditional religion and religious people—so biased that she will never willingly investigate the Christian gospel. Given her strong biases and emotional distaste for people who (as she sees it) "peddle their religion on street corners," how will we reach Judith with the Story of Jesus Christ?

Let's start with one indisputable fact: These days, God and His people have an image problem. A *serious* image problem. It is a problem that has been brought about, to a large degree, by people who advertise themselves as Christians but who, by their way of life and their witnessing style, betray the lifestyle and witnessing style of Christ Himself. As a result, many people in our culture—people just like Judith—are hindered from receiving the gospel because of their mental image of what "Christians" are like. Their stereotypes of Christians include such ideas as:

- Christians are bigoted, narrow-minded, and insincere.
- Christians are judgmental and enjoy making other people feel guilty, afraid, and uncomfortable.
- Christians try to convert by emotionalism, manipulation, and harassment.

Both clergy and laypeople find themselves increasingly "typecast" by these stereotypes. So when we share our Story with others, their reply is often, "You have nothing to say to me. I have no reason to listen to you or your Story."

Yet the very fact that postmodern men and women reject stereotyped "religion" because it lacks grace and authenticity should tell us something important: People who reject inauthentic "religion" are demonstrating that they are *hungry* for authentic *grace*. If we can demonstrate the authentic grace of Jesus Christ to tough skeptics like Judith, they will be convinced—and they will respond.

But how? How can we demonstrate grace to people like Judith?

Answer: By not only telling but actively *modeling* the Story of grace.

GRACE FOR THE UNFORGIVEN

Has the Story (with a big *S*) touched the story of your life? It has touched mine.

Grace has not always been an easy concept for me. I grew up

with a strong sense of perfectionism. As a boy I didn't excel in sports, so I compensated by turning to academic pursuits. In elementary school, I was an excellent speller. But by the age of nine or ten, I was already so driven by perfectionist tendencies that I dissolved in tears after missing one word in a spelling contest. In high school, I pursued courses in public speaking. I won an oratory contest at fifteen and began speaking to youth groups at the age of sixteen. Being a perfectionist, however, I tended to overprepare my speeches, and they lacked spontaneity. When I was successful in academic and speaking pursuits, I felt good about myself; but any little mistake put a stain on my sense of self-worth.

As I entered adulthood, I continued to set high standards for my life. When I failed to measure up to those standards, I was very hard on myself. Intellectually, I knew what grace was. I could recite the theological definition of grace, and I had memorized the mnemonic device to remind me that GRACE means God's Riches At Christ's Expense. I knew that salvation was by grace, not of works, so that no one has a right to boast of his or her own righteousness (as Ephesians 2:8-9 makes clear). But at a deep, emotional level, I needed to realize more of what grace really meant. For many years, any sense of achievement would be followed by periods of self-doubt.

In 1975, I had just such an experience several months after serving as program chairman of the historic Lausanne '74 Congress. I was scheduled to speak at an evangelistic crusade in Tulsa, Oklahoma. I should have felt charged up and exhilarated, but for reasons that are still hard for me to understand, I experienced a terrible sense of letdown and defeat as I approached Tulsa.

The first few nights of the crusade, I would get up to speak and the crowds would be very responsive. Yet, I felt I had nothing to say, nothing that could help anyone, nothing that would even be interesting. I wondered why any of those people would want to hear me. Each day of the crusade, my depression and self-doubt grew. Finally, I awoke one morning full of dread. I was supposed to go to the University of Tulsa that morning to speak at an open-air gathering of students, but I was so paralyzed with panic and depression I could hardly move. I wondered what the students would think of me; surely, everyone would see right through me and know that I had nothing to offer, nothing of value to say.

I prayed, "God, I don't think I can go out there! What do I do?" As I prayed, I remembered the words God had spoken to Abram in Genesis 15: "Do not be afraid, Abram. I am your shield, your very great reward." I felt God telling me, "Don't be afraid, Leighton, I'll be your shield, I'll protect you, I'll be there with you."

But God's promise of protection was only part of the insight I received in those moments. He had also told Abram, "I am . . . your very great reward." I had been a public speaker since age sixteen, and in all those years, most of my identity—my "reward"—was tied up in being a communicator. Now, as I was barraged with doubts about my value as a communicator, I was losing my identity. God was saying to me, "Trust Me. You matter to Me, not because you are Leighton Ford the communicator, but because you are My son, regardless of your performance."

I got up and went out to speak. I was really shaky, but God was with me. That was one of many experiences in my life that have forced me to question who I am, and that have driven me back to the grace of God. And I'm still learning.

I saw that same growth toward grace in the life of our older son Sandy. During the first fourteen years of his life, Sandy was much like me in his approach to grace—or perhaps I should say, in his retreat from grace. Throughout those early years, his focus was on becoming a good boy, an example of Christian behavior and virtue. He was the Puritan in our family. He'd always tell his sister if her bathing suit was too skimpy.

But at age fourteen, something happened to Sandy that transformed his understanding of God's grace: Sandy underwent his first heart surgery for a life-threatening arrythmia. For a time, he was unable to do anything for himself or for others. He was unable to perform good works for God. He faced a fact that few people his age ever have to think about: his own mortality and the brevity and preciousness of life. He experienced love from his family, from friends, and from God while flat on his back recuperating from open-heart surgery. He discovered that he was loved just for who he was, not for his behavior and his good works. In the last seven years of his life, I saw Sandy grow from a driven, perfectionist Puritan into a godly young man—and it was his discovery of grace that made all the difference. As a father, I've also watched with concern and gratitude as Debbie and Kevin too have learned the gift of grace at crucial points in their own journeys.

So as I reflect on the drivenness of my own life and the life of my son Sandy, I feel a strong sense of emotional identification with the people of our own postmodern generation. They are, in large part, a driven and unforgiven generation, a generation that desperately hungers for the touch of God's grace. Some have tried to invent their own religion—a religion of good works and good behavior and high achievement—yet they become discouraged when they realize they cannot meet the perfectionist standards they have set for themselves. They feel guilty and unforgiven, and they end up in therapy and support groups.

Others of our postmodern generation go in the opposite direction: Having thrown off the restraints of traditional morality and values, they eventually reach a point of dissatisfaction with their lives. They realize that in their selfish quest for ego gratification and material accumulation, they have left a trail of pain and regret—and they ultimately feel guilty and unforgiven.

The 1993 Western *Unforgiven*, directed by and starring Clint Eastwood, is a dark parable of the driven, unforgiven mood of our postmodern age. It is a grim and gritty film, and it accurately portrays the pain and emptiness of a human heart in need of grace. Eastwood plays an aging gunslinger named Bill Munny. In his younger, wilder days, Munny had killed many men. But as the film opens, we meet a Bill Munny who is no longer a gunslinger. He has been reformed by the love of a good woman, his wife, Claudia. It was Claudia who got him to give up whiskey and hang up his guns, but now Claudia is dead, killed by smallpox. Grieving, poor, and debt-ridden, Munny tries to eke out a living for himself and his two children as a pig farmer on the Texas plains.

Then one day, a brash young gunslinger calling himself "the Schofield Kid" rides up and reminds Bill Munny of his ugly past. "I hear you've killed a lot of men," the Kid tells him. "Well, up in Wyoming, there's a thousand dollars to be had for killing two cowboys. Seems those boys went into a whorehouse one night and one of 'em got mad at the woman he was with and he slashed up her face. The other ladies in that establishment have posted a bounty on the heads of those two cowboys. If you come with me, we can kill those boys and split that reward."

"No," Munny replies, honoring the wishes of his dead wife. "No more killin' for me. I ain't like that anymore."

The Kid rides off alone, but then Munny begins to think: *How are my children going to live? How will I pay off this debt? My split of that thousand dollars would sure go a long way.*

So he straps on his gun and rides out to catch up with the Schofield Kid. As they ride together, the Kid—who is fascinated by Munny's reputation as a killer—pumps him for stories of his past. Like the time he shot a cattle drover through the mouth and his teeth came out the back of his head. Or the time he shot three deputies who were trying to arrest him. Or the time he blew up a train. But Munny doesn't want to remember the sins of his past. "I ain't like that anymore," he keeps repeating to the Kid, and to himself, denying the obvious question: If he "ain't like that anymore," why is he riding to Wyoming to kill a couple of cowboys?

Together, Munny and the Kid track down the two cowboys. Munny shoots one of them, a fresh-faced boy named Davey, in a canyon. It's a grisly scene in which the boy dies slowly and painfully. Later, the Kid shoots the other cowboy—Quick Mike, the one who actually wielded the knife that cut the prostitute—while he's in the outhouse at the Bar T Ranch. It's a coldblooded killing of an unarmed man.

Later, the killings accomplished, Munny and the Kid sit under a tree outside of town, waiting for the prostitutes to send out their reward money. While they wait, they talk. The Kid is full of remorse, on the verge of tears. His earlier fascination with killing has evaporated, now that he has actually killed a man himself. But Munny, whose soul is stained with the blood of countless people, says, "Terrible thing, killing a man. You take away all he's got and all he's ever gonna have."

"Yeah," says the Kid, his voice choking. "Well, I guess they had it comin'."

Munny looks back at him coldly, then says, "We *all* have it comin', Kid."

It's a dark moment in a dark film, and there is even more blood-letting to come. Munny's terse comment—"We *all* have it comin'"—is the statement of a man who cannot escape his past, his sin, or his guilt. It's the statement of a damned soul.

The title is fitting: *Unforgiven*. For this is a film about guilt and retribution. Everyone in the film is guilty. The two dead cowboys are guilty of cutting up a prostitute. The prostitutes are guilty of offering blood money to killers, and setting in motion the machinery of revenge. The sadistic sheriff, played by Gene Hackman, is guilty. The Schofield Kid is guilty. And Bill Munny is guilty. In the end, everyone is guilty, and no one is forgiven.

And the question that occurs to the Christian mind as we view this parable of sin and unforgiveness is: "What if grace had come into that aging gunslinger's life? What if he could know grace and forgiveness?" But there is no grace, no forgiveness. Bill Munny is a man who cannot forgive, and who cannot be unforgiven. He is a symbol of the cycle of guilt and retribution that fuels the wars and killings we see in our own postmodern world: the Los Angeles riots, Middle East terrorism, religious strife in Northern Ireland, ethnic cleansing in Bosnia, and on and on and on.

That's why the Story of a God of grace is so important today. People all around us are drowning in guilt or hatred, convinced they are unforgiven, that they "have it comin'." They need to hear the Story you and I have to tell: the Story of the grace of the Son.

BLINDED BY THE LIGHT OF GRACE

The Story of God is the story of grace. We tend to think of the Old Testament as a book of law and the New Testament as a book of grace. Yet the truth is that the Story of God's grace begins in Genesis, where God graces this fallen world with people such as Noah, Abraham, and Moses, and where He foreshadows the coming of the Son. The Story of grace continues with David, who—after yielding himself to the sins of lying, adultery, and murder—is given a second chance by the forgiving grace of God. The Story unfolds throughout the Old Testament, which shows a patient, loving God giving grace to the entire nation of Israel. Finally, the Story of God's grace culminates in the central event of human history, when God graciously offers His only Son to rescue fallen men and women from their sin. From Genesis to Revelation, the Bible reveals to us a loving God who draws near to this world through the grace of His Son.

But the biblical story of grace I want to focus on is the story of a man with an obsession. He was a hardened, hateful religious teacher who had dedicated his life to destroying the first-century church. While God was moving through that church and expanding His Story of grace, this man was doing everything he could to stamp out that Story. His name was Saul.

If you had told the preconversion Saul that he would one day fall prostrate at the feet of Jesus, he would have laughed at you— or he might have even spat at you. But one day, on the road to Damascus, Saul met Jesus in a blinding experience of God's grace— and the unthinkable happened. It was high noon on the Damascus road when a blinding light flashed from Heaven, and a voice said, "Saul, why are you persecuting Me?"

"Who are you, Lord?" asked Saul in amazement.

The answer from Heaven: "I am Jesus."

Saul had spent his life studying about God. He was a Pharisee, a rabbi, a teacher—and suddenly he felt that he didn't know who God was at all! God was not the great, unforgiving destroyer he had thought He was. Rather, Saul discovered that God is the great Restorer. The last thing Saul ever expected was that Jesus was alive and that He would choose to speak to him!

And what did Jesus say to him? Saul might have expected Jesus to say, "Saul, I condemn you! Saul, I'll get even with you! Saul, I'm going to make you sorry for the way you've been persecuting My people!"

But that's not what Jesus said to Saul. Instead, Jesus did the unexpected. He extended an *invitation* to Saul: "I want you on My side, as a part of My redeemed community." Saul learned that day that Jesus was the Lord, Jesus was alive, and that Jesus—in His infinite grace—wanted *him!* On that road, Saul was struck blind by the light of grace. He was no longer able to see the world as he once did. For three days, Saul was sightless—and then God opened his eyes and gave him a new Vision. It was a Vision of the grace of Jesus, and that Vision exploded Saul's soul and transformed his life. No longer was he Saul the hardened Pharisee. His character was transformed, so that he became Paul, the Christian apostle, the missionary of grace.

As you read Paul's later writings, you see that he piles up word after word, picture after picture, in an effort to somehow express what grace has meant in his life. To the Philippians, he writes (and I paraphrase), "Christ Jesus took hold of me—it was as if He arrested me, apprehended me on that road! I was out to arrest the Christians, but He arrested me!"[1]

To the Corinthians, he writes, "For God, who said, 'Let light shine out of darkness,' made his light shine in our hearts to give us the light of the knowledge of the glory of God in the face of Christ."[2] In other words, "It was like at the very beginning of the universe, when God said, 'Let there be light!' He did it all over again! God said, 'Let there be light!' in my soul, and He made it shine in my heart!"

To Timothy, he writes, "The grace of our Lord was poured out on me abundantly."[3] I've stood in the North Carolina mountains and watched the heavens open and the rain just pour down, drenching the land. I've seen the floods rush down the gulleys and streambeds until they overflowed bridges and washed away roads, and I've thought, *That's what Paul was saying to Timothy: "The grace of God was like a torrent that overflowed and rushed over my soul!"*

Grace became the core of Paul's life and the kernel of his theology. Grace is what made a believer, a disciple, and a witness out of Paul. That's why he wrote, "For it is by grace you have been saved, through faith,"[4] and, "For the grace of God that brings salvation has appeared to all men."[5] When grace struck Saul/Paul like a thunderbolt there on the Damascus road, Saul's terrible obsession—his fanatical zeal to destroy the church—was instantly erased. In its place was a *magnificent* obsession. In that moment, the Story of God's grace collided with the story of Saul and called his story into question. Then God graciously reassembled Saul into a transformed man—a man He could use to achieve His purposes in history and in human lives. From Jerusalem to Judea to Samaria and out to the uttermost parts of the earth, God dramatically used this transformed man to expand His Kingdom and build His church. The vision of grace that Paul received on the road to Damascus transformed his character so that he became the very personification of evangelism. He became a natural storyteller and evangelist because *he could not help but tell the Story* wherever he went. The Story of God's grace was woven into his being and written upon his life, and those who saw him saw the Story of God. Paul's conversion story is such a powerful demonstration of the grace of Jesus Christ that he tells this story *three times* in the book of Acts, and makes frequent reference to it in his epistles.

The story of Paul is yet another illustration of this principle: *The Story produces a Vision, and the Vision transforms Character.*

It is the transformed character of Christians that convinces people of the truth of our Story. It is the transformed character of Christians that communicates the grace of God to a world that is drowning in guilt, feeling unforgiven and cut off from God. The good news of the grace of the Son was summed up by Charles Haddon Spurgeon, who wrote, "You *do* need a mediator between yourselves and God but you *do not* need a mediator between yourselves and Christ. You may come to him just as you are." That is what the people around us are aching and yearning to hear—and that is the Story you and I have to tell.

OUR STORY: THE GRACE OF THE SON

I was out of my office on the Friday afternoon when the call came from my grandson, Graham, so I received one of those pink "While You Were Out" notes. I called Graham back and said, "Hey, Graham, this is Gagee."

Graham, who was about six at the time, said, "Hi, Gagee! Guess what?"

"What, Graham?"

"I asked Jesus to come into my heart today."

I said, "That's great!" I knew that Graham's mother had been frustrated with his behavior, and I was pretty sure she had been talking to him lately about his need for grace and forgiveness!

But then Graham went on to say something that surprised me.

"Yeah, I asked Jesus into my heart today, but He didn't come in."

"He didn't?"

"No."

"How do you know that?"

"I didn't feel anything *move*."

"Well, you don't need to feel anything move, Graham. You just accept Jesus and believe Him when He says He will come into your life. You may not feel any different, but He'll be there all the same."

But Graham was adamant. "No, He didn't come in."

"Well, I'll come over Sunday and we'll talk."

So I went over Sunday afternoon and went up to Graham's room, and we played a bit and talked a bit. Then we started talking about his experience of praying. Graham was still convinced he had asked Jesus to come in and Jesus didn't come in. Throughout our visit, I prayed that God would give me the wisdom to somehow convey the grace of Jesus to my grandson.

At one point in our talk, I quoted to him Jesus' words from Revelation 3:20—"Here I am! I stand at the door and knock. If anyone hears my voice and opens the door, I will come in and eat with him, and he with me." (If you're a Bible scholar, you may object, "But that's not an evangelistic verse!" Still, it's a beautiful picture of Jesus waiting to be invited into our human lives—and with your grandson, you fudge a little to make a point!)

So Graham thought about that picture of Jesus standing outside the door of his heart, and then he said, "Gagee, you know what? I feel like there's a big piece of wood across the door, and Jesus can't get past that piece of wood and into my heart." I was amazed! This six-year-old boy had correctly analyzed a spiritual truth that many grownups never seem to grasp: Graham understood that there was a blockage between himself and God—and the blockage was on *his* side of the door, not God's. That blockage was sin.

But what Graham needed to understand—what so many people need to understand—is that the grace of Jesus is greater than the blockage of sin that bars the door of our hearts. So I said, "Graham, do you know what happened when Jesus died? He took that piece of wood and He just *exploded* it off that door!"

Graham looked up at me for a moment and his face lit up and he said, "Really?!"

I said, "Yes!"

Graham jumped up and ran downstairs to his mommy and daddy, and I heard him excitedly explain his new spiritual insight to them: "And—and—and that piece of wood just *blew* off that door!" And from that time on, Graham has known that Jesus is in his life. The revelation he encountered was *grace*, the grace of the Son, exploding off that cross, shattering the barriers between himself and God.

But is that the story we're telling to our own lost generation today?

A CLEAR, CLEAN STORY LINE

We pragmatic North American Christians often assume we know what the gospel is, and that we just need to get it out more effectively. I'm not so sure we do know—or that we can express the gospel Story clearly. Just think of all the "gospels" that are told and sold today:

- The "name it and claim it" gospel of wealth and health and success.
- The gospel of narcissistic self-affirmation: "I'm worth it," or even, "I am God."
- The gospel of right-wing political salvation.
- The gospel of left-wing political salvation.
- The gospel of twelve steps to recovery.

Will the story we tell in the 1990s and beyond have a clean, clear story line? Will we communicate the gospel Story as clearly and simply as Jesus Himself did?

This is not to say there may not be many story lines that make up the great Story of God. Nor do I want to suggest any criticism of any of the following:

- A healthy view of ourselves as people created in God's image.

■ A sense of responsibility toward our society and its problems.

■ Involvement in our political process.

■ The recovery movement and its efforts to liberate men and women from their addictions and compulsions.

These attitudes and actions are not foreign to grace, but they should not be substituted for the gospel of grace. Rather, they are the fruit of grace, the result of grace. When grace has entered our lives, we receive a healthy self-image, because we become children of the King and heirs of His Kingdom. When grace has entered our lives, our social and political involvement become extensions of our Christian faith and ministry for God. When grace has entered our lives, we truly understand who the "Higher Power," the "God of our understanding" named in the twelve steps of Alcoholics Anonymous (AA), is: Jesus Christ.

Peter is a friend of mine who is very much involved in Alcoholics Anonymous. He is the former director of a horse-racing track in Albuquerque. He lived his life in an alcoholic blur from age sixteen to age thirty-two. Then he found AA. At the age of forty-six, Peter met Jesus Christ in a personal way.

Peter tells me it's not easy to bring Christ into an AA meeting. "A lot of believers try to witness very bluntly about Jesus in the meetings," he says. "They mean well, but the AA traditions are very clear: There is to be no preaching, no proselytizing in the meetings. When people get preachy about Jesus, the leader will just say, 'Next,' and not call on that person again."

So Peter has learned to tell his story creatively. "Grace," he says, "is a big word in AA. I'll say, 'Life isn't fair, is it? We all complain that "there ain't no justice." But I don't want justice! I want mercy! If I got justice for everything I've done in my life, I'd be dead or in jail!' Or I'll say, 'I feel like a big blob of mud on the wheel a potter uses. I can't make anything of my life. I just sit there on the wheel like an inert mass. Then, when God goes to work, He shapes me into something He can use.' When I say things like that, heads nod.

"After the meeting, a few people will come over to me and

say, 'I don't know exactly everything you meant when you were speaking, but it sounded good and it rings true. Here's my card. Can we get together and talk?' And when we get together, we're not in an AA meeting, so I can name my Higher Power. And the name I name is Jesus Christ."

So the clear, clean story line of the gospel must be central to all that we do and say. No other story is *the* Story of God's grace. The gospel Story itself is "grace and peace." It is the Story that Jesus died and is alive and loves us (whether our self-esteem is high or low). It is the Story that Jesus is Lord, regardless of who is in the White House or the Congress. It is the Story of the One who "though he was rich, yet for your sakes he became poor, so that you through his poverty might become rich."[6] It is the Story of a God who moves toward us and meets us right where we are. It is the simple yet profound Story of a God who loves us so much that He gave us His only Son. We don't have to clean ourselves up or improve ourselves before God is willing to meet us: the cleaning and the improving is up to Him. All we have to do, according to God's grace, is receive the free gift He gives us.

At the same time, however, we should be careful never to communicate what Dietrich Bonhoeffer called a gospel of "cheap grace." The grace of God is costly; it cost the Son untold suffering and death upon the cross. And grace can be painful to you and me as well. But the pain that grace brings is a *healing* pain, the pain of self-appraisal, self-judgment, and confession. Grace judges us in order to heal us. Grace does not wink at the sin in our lives; grace seeks to eradicate the sin from our lives so that we can be free. To truly appropriate the grace of the Son, we must face squarely the awfulness of our sin and recognize that it was our sin that nailed Jesus to the cross. As D. T. Niles, that great Sri Lankan Christian writer once said, "No one comes to himself until he can look at the cross and say, 'I did that to Him and He did that for me.'"

In twelfth-century Japan, two Buddhist priests, Honen and his disciple Shinran, came to a remarkable conclusion. "We cannot walk the eight-fold path of enlightenment and perfection by our own efforts. We cannot achieve Buddhahood by learning, meditation, rituals, or good deeds. Human effort is not enough to save us." So these two priests founded the Jodo sect of Buddhism.

The word *Jodo* means Pure Land—that is, *Heaven*. In fact, these two founders of the Jodo sect formulated a branch of Buddhism that looks remarkably like Christianity in many ways— *yet without Christ*. Honen and Shinran taught that Jodo, the Pure Land, could not be reached by human effort or righteousness, but only by faith in the deity they called Amida. Salvation and transformation, they said, takes place at the moment faith is first expressed. What is the basis, then, of salvation? And what is the focus of this faith? According to Honen and Shinran, the source of salvation and the focus of faith is the unearned, merciful favor of Amida, gratefully accepted as a free gift. We Christians readily recognize this concept as *grace*.

But where did these teachings come from? Why are they so similar to Christian teachings while lacking the most important feature of Christianity, Christ Himself? No one knows.

In the early years of this century, one of the direct successors of Honen and Shinran, a priest of the Jodo sect, wrestled with the question, Where does grace come from? Why should Amida care about me and my needs? Why should Amida give me grace?

Eventually, this man was led to a Bible study at the Imperial University in Tokyo. There, for the first time in his life, this Buddhist priest read the story of Jesus the Son. After hearing the Story of the grace of the Son, this man said, "Now I understand where grace comes from! The connection is Jesus Christ, the Son of God." He gave his life to Christ and went on to write a tremendous book comparing the teachings of Buddha with the grace of Christ. This book has been published in Japanese but has not yet been translated into English.

There are many people like this Japanese priest, people of all cultures and religious backgrounds, scattered all around the world— and they are hungry for grace, the authentic life-changing grace of Jesus, the Son of God. They are hungering to hear the Story we have to tell. It is a Story that gives us a Vision of Jesus and the difference He can make in human lives. And that Vision should so transform our Character that we will be compelled to tell that Story at every opportunity to the hungering, grace-starved people around us.

OUR VISION: A VISION OF HEAVEN, A VISION OF GRACE

The Story creates a Vision. That's certainly what happened in the life of the Apostle Paul. Vance Havner, that grand old North Carolina country preacher, used to say that Paul's encounter with Christ on the Damascus road was a "Who-What" experience. His first question to Jesus was "*Who* are you, Lord?" and his follow-up question was "Lord, *what* do you want me to do?" Grace demanded a response from Paul.

Later in his ministry, Paul appeared before King Agrippa and told his story: "I heard a voice saying . . . , 'I am Jesus. . . . I have appeared to you to appoint you as a servant and as a witness of what you have seen of me'"—that is, Paul's *Vision*—"'and what I will show you'"—that is, the *Vision* to come. "So then, King Agrippa," Paul continued, "I was not disobedient to the *vision* from heaven."[7] As Christians, most of us are familiar with Paul's conversion story. Yet I wonder if we fully realize how that shattering encounter on the Damascus road solidified the heart of Paul's theology and shaped his approach to evangelism for the rest of his life. That Vision of Jesus was the central pillar of his powerful apostolic ministry and of his forceful personality.

As we look at Paul's evangelistic ministry through a narrative lens, we gain a new understanding of what evangelism means. Under the old paradigm, evangelism is something we do: a task, a job, a program, a burden, an expectation, a venture, a challenge. But under the new paradigm of narrative evangelism, evangelism is not merely what we do, but *who we are*. If our Vision transforms our Character, then we can't help but be witnesses to God's grace. Telling the Story of God's grace will be as natural as breathing.

You and I may not have experienced the kind of dramatic conversion that Paul did on the road to Damascus, yet the reality of God's grace is as real in our lives as it was in his. As we meditate and immerse ourselves in the Story of God's grace, as it has touched our lives, our Vision of His grace will be expanded, and our Character will be transformed—and the result will be that the Story of God will be indelibly engraved upon our lives and our behavior for all around us to see. Our witnessing will not just be the result of a program, it will be part of the very texture of our lives.

What is Jesus' vision for evangelism throughout the world? Throughout North America? Throughout our neighborhoods and our own families?

Is it His vision that everyone will hear the Story of God and of His grace? Of course it is.

And is it His vision that people will leave self-centered living and turn to God? Yes! He is not willing that any should perish, but that all would repent and turn to Him.

Is it His vision that churches will be planted and grow? Absolutely!

Is it His vision that a new community will be formed, a transformed community where people of all backgrounds and ethnicities and personality types will merge and blend? A place where orthodox and progressive, white and black, Asian and Hispanic, male and female can find grace and peace with God and with each other in Jesus? Yes!

Now the question that confronts you and me is this: Is His Vision *our* Vision? And has this Vision transformed our Character?

OUR CHARACTER: THE GRACE OF THE SON MODELED IN OUR LIVES

One of the greatest challenges we face as we seek to be witnesses in a post-Christian, postmodern age is that few people are willing to sit still and listen to our Story. People want to be entertained. Not instructed, not challenged, not preached to, but *entertained*.

As communications professor Neil Postman has observed in his book *Amusing Ourselves to Death*, we have moved from an age of exposition to an age of entertainment. He explains that the previous age was a literate age, an age when people absorbed their entertainment through reading. For example, when novelist Charles Dickens came to the U.S. in 1841, he received the kind of tumultuous welcome that would greet a rock star today, because the people of that generation were readers.

Postman also notes that people in the literate age of exposition were willing to sit patiently through long speeches, listening to lecture, debate, and teaching. When Abraham Lincoln and

Stephen Douglas argued the issue of slavery, they often debated for as long as seven hours at a time. But today we want all our information condensed, predigested, and accompanied by pictures and graphs. We have become increasingly visual rather than verbal in our preferences. We spend less and less of our time reading, and more and more of our time viewing.

One indicator of the decreasing attention span of our society came in 1992, during the U.S. presidential campaign. The television networks had received a great deal of criticism in previous campaigns for reducing the national political debate to a series of nightly seven- or eight-second "sound bites"—taped segments in which the presidential candidates explained their positions in their own words. So, in an attempt to make its coverage appear more substantial, CBS News made a major announcement: It was going to increase the average length of its sound bites from seven to twenty-four seconds—as if the major issues of our nation could be adequately addressed in twenty-four seconds!

It would be easy to cast stones at the news media for trivializing our national debate—but could it be that we in the church have committed the same offense by trivializing the gospel? Postman suggests that we in the church have turned the Christian faith into just another form of entertainment. Christian books, Christian television, Christian music, and even Christian worship services have become just part of the larger entertainment business. The goal, in many Christian quarters, is not to change lives but to hold an audience and turn a profit.

Jesus did not intend His church merely to provide bigger and better amusement for bigger and more upscale audiences. His Vision was of a church that would inject His light and life into a dark and dying world. So we had better take the Vision of Jesus seriously, or we won't just be amusing ourselves to death. We'll be amusing people to hell.

I'm not suggesting that churches should be dull and dry. Quite the opposite. The "seeker-friendly" worship services pioneered by such churches as Willow Creek Community Church in the Chicago area have created a lively, exciting atmosphere where people "on their way back to God" can hear the Story of God in an inviting setting. Many churches today offer baby boomers and baby busters a blend of contemporary music, dance, drama, and preaching that combines biblical truth with storytelling techniques, including wit and comedy. InterVarsity Christian Fellowship uses actor Bruce Kuhn on campuses to vividly narrate Luke's story of Jesus. The creative and innovative approaches to telling the Story of God can be very effective means of evangelism.

But all too often, in our attempts to "sell" the gospel as a television show or a product in a Christian bookstore, we have watered down the truth of the Story of God. And this we must never do. Instead we must find a bridge between entertainment and exposition, between what people want to see and what people desperately need to hear. I am convinced that the bridge between entertainment and exposition is *narrative*, the act of *storytelling*. In fact, I see narrative evangelism as the new way of exposition. Instead of telling the gospel Story by expounding and exegeting the biblical texts in a sentence-by-sentence fashion, we must bring the truth of God alive just as Jesus did, with stories, parables, word pictures, and vivid metaphors. Even Bible "word-studies" can be put in story and word-picture language!

One of the greatest American storytellers of all time was Herman Melville, the author of *Moby Dick*. Those who knew Melville personally, such as fellow novelist Nathaniel Hawthorne, could testify that Melville was just as good a storyteller in person as he was on paper. One night, Hawthorne and his wife, Sophia, invited Melville to dine with them at their home in western Massachusetts. After dinner, Melville—who had spent several years as a crewman on a whaling ship—regaled his hosts with a story of a terrible battle he once witnessed on an island in the South Pacific. As he described the action of the battle, he swung about with both arms, imitating the actions of the club-wielding island warriors. Hawthorne and his wife were spellbound throughout the tale.

Later, after Melville left their home, Hawthorne said to his wife, "Herman forgot it!"

"What did he forget?" asked Sophia.

"That carved club he was swinging as he told that story about the battle in the South Pacific!"

"Oh, that!" said Sophia, remembering the club. "Let's find it and you can take it to him tomorrow."

So they looked and looked for the club, but after a full hour of searching were unable to locate it.

The next day, Hawthorne went to see Melville and said to him, "Herman, we have looked all over the house and can't find your club anywhere!"

"Club?" asked Melville. "What club?"

"The club you were swinging when you told us about your adventure in the South Seas! You forgot to take it home with you."

Melville spread his hands in bewilderment. "But I had no club!"

Melville was telling the truth. His story was so vivid in the minds of Nathaniel and Sophia Hawthorne that they *believed* they had seen a club in his hands! That's the power of storytelling. It creates living pictures in people's minds, and brings events and truths to life.

And that is the challenge before you and me as storytellers of God's grace: As we tell and live out His Story in our daily lives, we must make the grace and truth of Jesus Christ so vivid that it can be *seen* and *touched* by the minds and imaginations of the people around us.

In 1992, I met with leaders of fifty-five denominations in Chicago, and our primary purpose in meeting was to covenant together and commit ourselves to the goal that *every person in the U.S.* would have a clear picture of Jesus and His grace by the end of the twentieth century. There is much biblical illiteracy and much misunderstanding of who Jesus was and what the gospel is about. Many people still labor under the misconception that the way to salvation is to live a good enough life or to undergo certain religious rituals. Despite its clear, clean simplicity, the concept of the grace of the Son is still a tragically misunderstood idea. But what if you and I and every other evangelical Christian would plan and pray and use every opportunity to convey to the people around us a clear picture of Jesus and His grace?

And *how* will we convey this picture of Jesus and His grace to the people around us? We have already seen that the present generation does not have the patience or the inclination to be preached to. Ours is a visual, not verbal, generation. The people around us don't want to be *told* what is true; they want to *see* the truth with their own eyes. So how do we tell the Story of grace to those around us? We tell it in a visible, active, living way. We tell this Story with our lives, and above all, with our *Character*.

The Story creates a Vision, and the Vision must produce Character. The Character we display to those around us is the clearest, cleanest, most convincing witness we have. When our Character is seen to be consistent with our Story, then our voice will be clear, and our Story will be heard.

CHAPTER TEN

A TOUCH OF GRACE

VOICE AND TOUCH TOGETHER

Max DePree is the CEO of Herman Miller, Inc., and a nationally known speaker and writer on the subject of leadership. He tells a story from his own experience that vividly demonstrates the power of a literal, physical touch of grace.

Soon after DePree's married daughter became pregnant, her husband moved out and abandoned her. So she was alone when the baby was born about four months prematurely. "I went to the hospital to see my new grandchild for the first time," DePree recalls, "and there in that incubator was a tiny little baby, about the size of my hand, with wires running from his body to a lot of monitors and machines."

As he was watching his grandchild silently struggle for life, the senior nurse went to him and said, "Mr. DePree, that baby's father isn't here, so for the next several months, you will have to be the baby's surrogate father. Here's what I want you to do. When you visit the baby, go to the incubator, put your hand through the cuffs, and stroke the child. As you touch the child with your hands, talk to the child. It's very important that he experiences your voice and your touch together."

Voice and touch—together.

That is how our gospel must be communicated. The Story of God's grace must not only be told in words. If we want to reach Judith and people like her, we must *model* an evangelism of grace. We must communicate not only with a clear *voice*, but with the authentic *touch* of grace. Our evangelism must be a *hands-on* evangelism, in which we roll up our sleeves and dare to touch human lives. Our voice must be clear and our touch must be real—as real as the touch of Ananias.

Again we return to the conversion of the Apostle Paul, to witness the crucial role that was played by a man named Ananias, one of the unsung heroes of the early Church. When God told Ananias to go to Saul, Ananias protested, "Lord, I have heard many reports about this man and all the harm he has done to your saints in Jerusalem. And he has come here with authority from the chief priests to arrest all who call on your name." It seemed to Ananias that God was sending him on a suicide mission! Yet Ananias obediently responded to the call of the Lord, and he went to the house where Saul waited, still blind from his encounter on the Damascus road.

And what did Ananias do when he met Saul? He *touched* him: "Placing his hands on Saul, [Ananias] said, 'Brother Saul, the Lord—Jesus, who appeared to you on the road as you were coming here—has sent me so that you may see again and be filled with the Holy Spirit.' Immediately, something like scales fell from Saul's eyes, and he could see again."[1] Ananias's act of obedience was an amazing demonstration of Christian courage, and his first words to Saul—the sworn enemy of all Christians!—was a powerful demonstration of Christian hope!

Soon after Saul received his sight, he was baptized and joined the disciples, becoming one of the most effective missionaries of all time. But the intermediary of God's grace to Saul was a *touch*—the two hands of Ananias, laid upon the head of this baby Christian. From Ananias, Paul experienced the literal, physical *touch* of grace.

The model of Ananias is *our* model. God calls us, as story-tellers of His Story of grace, to move toward people, to reach out to people, to place our hands on people, to give them the touch of grace. How, in a practical sense, do you touch the lives of others with the grace of the Son? You touch the people around you when-ever you:

- Roll up your sleeves and lend a hand to the new neighbors who are trying to wrestle a refrigerator into the apartment next door.
- Stop to help the bedraggled-looking woman whose car is broken down beside the road, whose children are crying, who doesn't know where to turn or what to do for help.
- Attend the funeral of your coworker's mother, so that you can put your arm around him and show him you care.
- Offer to keep your neighbors' children for the weekend so they can get away for some long-overdue time with each other.
- Get a group of Christian friends together to clean the yard and paint the house of the woman across the street, who is worn out from caring for her aging mother at home.

In short, you offer the touch of God's grace whenever you lend your presence and your practical, helping touch to people with a hurt or a need. You may say, "But that's not evangelism!" And you are right. Evangelism is more than just touching lives and serving people. Evangelism must include both our *touch* and our *voice*—together.

Our touch cannot tell the Story; only our voice can do that. But the touch of grace makes the Story of grace come alive. It makes people's hearts receptive to the Story. It provokes curios-ity and interest in the Story. And it lends congruence and credi-bility to the Story. When we tell our Story by linking our touch and voice together, we practice the most powerful form of evan-gelism of all, because *this* witness is vital, visual, and active. It touches the throbbing pulse of human need.

As Bill Hybels, pastor of Willow Creek Community Church,

says, the practical touch of grace "unstereotypes" evangelism—both for us as Christians and for the people around us. It takes the fear out of sharing our faith with others. If the thought of witnessing to other people paralyzes you, if you object, "But I'm not an evangelist!"—then you should know that nothing could be simpler than giving a practical touch of grace to the people around you. You *can* be an evangelist just by offering to baby-sit or by jump-starting a car or by taking someone to lunch or by putting your arm around a person who is lonely and hurting.

But the practical touch of grace also "unstereotypes" evangelism for the people around us by cutting through all the objections people have about the Christian faith. Like our fictional friend Judith, many nonChristian people (or, I should say, *pre*-Christian people or, as a friend describes them, "Christologically challenged" people!) have negative stereotypes of Christians—stereotypes about what Christians are like, about what Christians say, about how Christians behave, about how Christians make other people feel. "Christians are all a bunch of hypocrites," is one of the most common complaints. But the practical touch of grace knocks down all those stereotypes. Here's how it works:

Stereotype 1: What Are Evangelists Like?
Take any group of mostly unchurched people and ask them to say the first words that come to mind when you say "Christian evangelist"—then stand back! I've performed this experiment many times with different groups, and more often than not the words that people think of are such negative terms as *pushy, aggressive, insensitive, close-minded, know-it-all, salesman, argumentative, talkative, arrogant,* and *annoying.*

But now try another experiment: Ask yourself, "Who is the one person most responsible for bringing me to Christ?" Picture that person in your mind, then think of one or two words that most characterize that person.

I have conducted this experiment with groups of people in seminars, universities, and churches in our own country and in many other parts of the world. Invariably, the words people think of include such positive terms as *caring, loving, humble, genuine, good listener, sensitive, fun to be around, patient*, and *accepting*. In other words, the people who tend to be the most influential in leading others to Christ are people who have a certain kind of Character. They are people who, like Jesus Christ Himself, are full of grace and truth. What does this say to us about the kind of people we should be, the kind of Character we should display, if we want to lead other people to Jesus Christ?

Stereotype 2: How Do Evangelists Make People Feel?

Ask most pre-Christians how evangelists make them feel, and they will likely use words such as *guilty, afraid, uncomfortable, defensive*, or *angry*. Of course, some people will react defensively or with guilt to even the most gracious presentation of the gospel, because they are resisting the probing of the Holy Spirit. But if we are honest, we have to acknowledge that it is often we, not the Holy Spirit, who cause people to feel uncomfortable. This is because we, as Christians, sometimes major more on the "bad news" than on the good news that God has sent us to tell.

Noted pastor-author-evangelist Lane Adams suggests that, for some, conversion is just a "switch of hostilities." When some of us come to Christ, we gain a new set of enemies, and we tend to "demonize" the opposition. We are quick to label other people as "proabortion" or "secular humanists" or "liberal." We get these people in our sights and we gun them down with our words. Instead of seeing them as people for whom Christ died, we see them as enemies to be defeated.

For all too many Christians, the gospel consists of, "I am right and you are wrong. Your lifestyle is wrong. Your values are wrong. Your beliefs are wrong. You are going to hell." The gospel is supposed to be *good* news, but the way many Christians proclaim it, it sounds like *bad* news! There is bad news about sin—but what we need to find is a good way to tell it—that there is a way out!

Lane Adams describes a fascinating fact he learned from Dr. Jack Haskins, director of the Graduate School of Communications at the University of Tennessee. Dr. Haskins had conducted a study on the impact of bad news on people. In his study, he discovered that if anyone hears a five-minute news broadcast with four bad news items, that listener will become (1) more depressed, (2) more negative, and (3) less inclined to help others. Heavy viewers/listeners of bad news tend to exhibit a growing belief that they will be the next victims of bad news. But that was not all Dr. Haskins discovered in his study. He found that people don't just get their bad news from *USA Today* and Dan Rather and CNN. He found that much of the depressing, negative information that bombards people comes from *Bible-believing Christians!* In fact, his research led him to conclude that the evangelical and fundamentalist wings of the church were among the greatest sources of negativism in the world today!

"That's not what God intended for His church or for evangelism," Lane Adams concludes. "God tells us that His promises are Good News, they are 'Yes' in Christ! [1 Corinthians 1:20]. How did we in the church get such a negative reputation when every promise we have in Christ is God's great affirmative 'Yes' in Jesus?" He's exactly right. Our message in Christ should be "Yes," a message of grace. When being a "Christian" means little more than being hostile to things that are "nonChristian," then our lives lack grace. We lose the opportunity to give the touch of grace to other people, and to evangelize them with the gracious character of our lives.

If we want to know how we, as Christian storytellers, should make people feel, we should look to our model, Jesus Himself. Yes, He could be tough and confrontational with the hypocrites and Pharisees, those who were oppressing the people. But with those He sought to *reach* with the good news—the sinners, the sick, the poor, the lonely—He was always gracious and His message was always "Yes!" In His dialogues with people like Nicodemus and the rich young ruler, Jesus demonstrated grace in the way He listened and responded courteously and attentively, and in the way He even respected their right to walk away. He was accepting and affirming of outcasts like Zaccheus, the despised tax collector, and the woman at the well. Jesus didn't just focus on His message, on making His point. He focused on *people*, on *their* feelings, on *their* needs, on *their* issues, on *their* healing. He made people feel valued and loved.

And so should we.

Stereotype 3: What Do Evangelists Say?

George Hunter suggests that, all too often, evangelism is "an unrequested and unnegotiated monologue, wherein the evangelizer controls the process, he is not generally interested in nor open to the other person, and gives the other no credit for knowing, believing, or having experienced anything worthwhile." All too often, evangelism means making a package presentation of the gospel, laden with religious jargon—"Are you born again? Are you washed in the blood of the Lamb?"—that means nothing to the average person in our culture.

But what is evangelism as God intended it to be? Gracious conversation! "Let your conversation be always full of grace, seasoned with salt," wrote the Apostle Paul, "so that you may know how to answer everyone."[2] Here again, our model is Christ Himself, of whom Luke records, "All spoke well of him and were amazed at the gracious words that came from his lips."[3] And our model is that of the early disciples, who learned directly from Jesus, and who, says the book of Acts, testified about Jesus with "great power" and "much grace."[4]

What, in practical terms, is "gracious conversation"? I would submit that *gracious* conversation is *two-way* conversation. I have asked many Christians how they were brought to Christ, what kind of person witnessed to them, and what kind of conversation they had. Again and again it has been confirmed to me that the person who witnesses most effectively tends to listen about 80 percent of the time and talk only about 20 percent of the time.

But this finding should not surprise us, because this is the model for effective evangelism that Jesus Himself gave us! Look closely at the story of Jesus' conversation with the woman at the well in John chapter 4. You will find that the woman speaks *four times* as many words as Jesus does. Jesus spends 80 percent of his time with this woman *just listening*.

For many Christians, evangelism means talking, telling the story, getting the point across. They talk. They expound. They interrupt. But they forget to *listen*. They may win arguments, but they don't win many people to Christ. If we want to demonstrate the grace of the Son to the people around us, we would do well to practice becoming a "big ear" rather than a "big mouth."

Yes, we must not hesitate to speak the truth when the opportunity presents itself. But our *truth* must go hand in hand with the *grace* of listening.

Another way we practice gracious conversation is by *asking permission* to tell our Story rather than simply charging in and imposing our Story on others. When I ask Christians how they were brought to Christ, one comment I frequently hear is: "The person who witnessed to me asked my permission to share the gospel. It was not an unrequested monologue. I didn't feel threatened or defensive by being buttonholed with the gospel. I felt valued and affirmed because this person was considerate of my time and my feelings."

Perry, a friend of mine who directs a ministry with men in South Carolina, tried for years to witness to his father about Jesus Christ. When Perry became a Christian at age sixteen, he ran home excitedly to share this good news with his father. But his father didn't want to hear about Jesus Christ. "I don't want you to talk about Jesus around the house," his father responded flatly. "I don't want you to discuss it with me, your mother, your brother, or any of our friends. It's a phase you're going through, and it will pass!"

Perry later went to college, then married and moved to a different state. Because his dad would not talk about Christ, Perry wondered how he could communicate the grace of Jesus to his father. Then he got an idea: *I'll write him a letter just as Paul wrote to the Romans, Galatians, and Corinthians—only I'll send one letter every month.* So every month, just like clockwork, Perry wrote to his dad. Perry spent about half of each letter talking about basic things that were going on in his life and half talking about the truths he was learning about Jesus and the Christian life. Sometimes, the "letter" was in the form of a cassette tape, and he would include the voices of his own children, hoping that a few words or baby sounds from the grandchildren would be just the touch to soften up his dad's heart when the gospel was shared. His dad never answered one of those letters or cassettes, or even acknowledged that he'd received them.

One month, Perry failed to write the usual monthly letter. As he sat studying at his desk, the phone rang. From the other end he heard, "Hey, where's my letter?" and then the phone was hung up.

"What kind of a nutty crank was that?" Perry wondered. Then it dawned on him that the voice was familiar. It was his dad! So Perry called back, "Dad, was that you on the phone?"

"Yes!" his dad responded. "Where is my letter?" Then he hung up again. Perry knew his dad was kidding around—but he also knew that his dad was serious about missing his usual letter! That was the first time Perry ever knew that his dad even read the letters, much less appreciated them!

So Perry called again. "Dad," he said, "I'm sorry I've been so wrapped up in my graduate studies lately. Besides, you never responded to my letters or tapes, so I had no way to know if they meant anything to you. After all, you're not really interested in spiritual things."

"No, I'm not," his father replied, "but I like getting your letters. I look forward to them every month. I've read each one and listened to all your tapes."

The next month Perry resumed his habit of writing to his dad.

Four years later, Perry's dad drove up the coast to visit his son. It was a good visit, in which the older man apologized for having been so harsh with Perry when he was sixteen. And then this unsaved man went on to give Perry some advice on effective witnessing. "Listen, Perry," he said, "when you're trying to witness to someone like me about the Lord, don't just come in and say your piece. Don't be like a used-car salesman. Ask permission. Let the other person control the conversation."

Perry told me later, after reflection, "My unsaved dad taught me a lot about witnessing, about gracious conversation. From then on, when I wanted to discuss spiritual things with my dad, I always opened with, 'Dad, could I share something with you?' And usually, he'd be fairly open to that."

Stereotype 4: What Do Evangelists Do?

The traditional stereotype of an evangelist is someone who stages a big event—say, under a tent or in a stadium—to which people come and sit as a captive audience. They listen to the evangelist preach and then, it is hoped, some will respond. Now, after my years of association with Billy Graham, I would be the last person to discount the effectiveness of well-planned, high-visibility mass evangelism. With adequate prayer, preparation, and presentation, these events can be powerful evangelistic opportunities—*if* the pre-Christians are there to respond to the message.

The problem is that pre-Christians are often not there. When that happens, these events become rallies where thousands of Christians gather together and the Story is preached to the converted. That is not bad, but it is not evangelism.

So how do we transcend the stereotype of what evangelists do? By living out the *reality* of gracious evangelistic action, by living a lifestyle of grace. Instead of only calling pre-Christian people to our events, these postmodern times also call us to *move toward* people and meet them where they are. This is how Jesus evangelized—meeting people on their own turf and on their own terms. This does not mean that the era of the well-planned evangelistic event is over. In fact, I believe that as Christians increasingly move toward pre-Christian people with an evangelism of grace, we will begin to see some of the more traditional forms of evangelism having an even deeper and broader impact than ever before.

In Matthew's understated account of his own conversion, we find a narrative of a celebration that I would like to see brought back into use today: a "salvation party." In that account, Matthew says Jesus approached him at his tax collector's booth and said, "Follow me," and Matthew followed. Then Matthew called all his friends together for a dinner party. He wanted his friends to meet this amazing man who had begun to change the direction of his life. And who did Matthew invite? Not the social elite and the leaders of the religious community! No, he invited the kind of people who generally hang out with tax collectors: other tax collectors, sinners, and social outcasts—the people of Matthew's decidedly unsavory social network. And there, in the midst of them, chatting and laughing and enjoying Matthew's "salvation party," was Jesus Himself!

The Pharisees, the religious elite of Matthew's day, didn't

approve of Jesus or this "salvation party," with its guest list of "lowlifes" and "riffraff." But Jesus' reply to the Pharisees was a statement of pure, unadulterated grace: "It is not the healthy who need a doctor, but the sick. . . . I have not come to call the righteous, but sinners."[5]

If we held "salvation parties" for the "sinners" and the "riffraff" of our own society, I'm sure there would be some high-minded Christian people who would object. But the all-encompassing grace of God silences all objections. There are many ways of inviting people to the Lord—if we will permit the Holy Spirit to move through His people, bringing about innovations and experiments with different approaches to evangelism; if we will expand our definition of what an evangelist is. I believe that when we hear the word *evangelist*, we shouldn't just think of people like Billy Graham or Luis Palau or Leighton Ford. We should also think of people like John and Boots Carter.

My friends the Carters practice what I call "Chinese water torture" evangelism. They evangelize drop by drop, little by little, as they make a gracious, caring difference in the lives of the people around them. They each have their own style, their own story. John is a great "testimonial" evangelist. He loves to tell how, after sixty years of being an "acting" Christian, he discovered what it means to be an "actual" Christian.

John's wife, Boots, is a great "relational" evangelist. She loves people warmly and graciously, invites them into her house, and captivates them with her hospitality. If the people she wants to reach are "cocktail party" people, then she will have a cocktail party—whatever it takes to bring people to a place where they can hear at least something of the grace of Jesus Christ. Some might not approve of "cocktail party evangelism," but my question to such people is this: "What is *your* strategy for reaching the people around you for Jesus Christ?"

Today, we have the freedom—and, I believe, the imagination—to evangelize in ways undreamed of by previous generations. Church growth strategist Lyle Schaller envisions "multiple ports of entry" by which pre-Christian people can come into the church and into God's Kingdom—and Schaller's vision is coming true in the 1990s.

It used to be that there were very few ports of entry into the church. In the early years of this century, one of the primary points of entry was the Sunday evening service, where pre-Christian people were invited to a service where the gospel was preached and an invitation was given. After World War II, the Sunday school emerged as a powerful evangelistic tool in most churches. From the mid-1960s to the 1980s, the Sunday morning worship service—especially the Willow Creek–style "seeker service"—was a principal point of entry.

But as we move through the 1990s, we are seeing a proliferation of entry points, especially nonweekend events such as cell groups and home Bible studies, retreats, support and recovery groups, athletic groups, and affinity groups. The church is finally saying to unchurched people, "The gospel is approachable and inviting, and it is for you, wherever you are, whatever your interest or your hurt or your need."

What do evangelists do? The stereotypical answer is, "They preach." But what do effective evangelists *really* do? They *touch*. Are we willing to touch people in their sin and pain and loneliness? Are we willing to give a touch of grace to the people that come into our lives every day? If we want our voice and our Story to be heard, we have to be willing to touch.

Voice and touch—together.

That is an evangelism of grace.

GRACE UNDER FIRE

The New Testament word for "witness" is *martus*, from which we derive our English word *martyr*. In fact, there are many places in the New Testament where the concept of a martyr is used interchangeably with that of a witness. Why? Because in the days of the early Church, it was expected that a witness for Christ would have to absorb the hostility of an anti-Christian world. Whenever a person witnessed, there was always martyrdom, self-sacrifice, abuse—and sometimes even death. That was accepted. Martyrdom just went with the territory. Many people saw the incredible *grace* that these early Christians displayed—a supernatural grace under fire—and they became convinced that the Story these Christians told and lived out was absolutely true. People were attracted to Christ by the grace of His suffering saints, and the church grew at an exponential rate.

The early Church's view of witnessing is foreign to most of us in the American church today. We think it strange and unfair for us to have to take criticism or persecution for the sake of the gospel. We say, "Poor us! Poor us! We're victims of a cruel and hostile world!" whenever we are ridiculed by our secular society or the liberal press. We are offended and outraged. We file grievances and organize boycotts because we resent being "victimized" by our post-Christian world—and thus we miss the blessings that God gives to those true martyrs who authentically suffer for the sake of His gospel.

Jesus said, "Blessed are you when people insult you, persecute you and falsely say all kinds of evil against you because of me."[6] But do we really believe that? Do we actually believe that we can be martyr-witnesses for Christ, patiently and prayerfully absorbing this world's hostility, accepting and forgiving this world's injustices toward us, so that we can point some person to Christ?

Tom Bowers is that kind of martyr-witness. He is married to my wife's niece, Cathy. Years ago, when Tom was a grad student at Wheaton College near Chicago, his sister, Margie, was working at nearby Moody Bible Institute. During this time, a mentally disturbed young man (who had spent time in a mental institution for killing someone during a psychotic episode) became obsessed with Margie's roommate, Esther. One night this troubled young man went to Margie's apartment to see Esther, but Esther wasn't there. Margie explained that Esther had just moved out to begin preparations for her wedding. The man flew into a rage, pulled a knife, and stabbed Margie thirty-seven times. He was later apprehended and imprisoned for the murder of Tom's sister, Margie.

Tom was devastated by the death of his sister. He and Margie had always been very close, and the horror and senselessness of her death left him with a huge knot of grief and anger inside. For fifteen years, those toxic emotions coursed through his soul. During that time, he married and moved to Charlotte, North Carolina, where he took an outside sales position.

One Friday afternoon, while driving home to North Carolina from a business trip in Virginia, Tom was thinking about a Bible study he would be leading the following Sunday. The subject: forgiveness. As he was going over the lesson in his mind, he felt an urging within him, almost like an audible voice. It was as if the Lord were saying to him, "You're going to teach about forgiveness? But Tom, what about Margie?"

"God really got hold of me that day," Tom recalls. "He just nailed my hide to the wall. The fact is, I had never forgiven the murderer of my sister. I knew I had to forgive—but I also knew I couldn't forgive. Not yet. I decided to put it off—but God wasn't going to let me off the hook."

That Sunday morning, Tom got up before the Sunday school class and spoke on forgiveness. It was an impersonal, abstract lesson—principles and concepts without any personal reality. Near the end of his presentation, Tom invited questions and discussion from the group. It soon became clear that people in the class were struggling to apply Tom's abstract teaching to their own experience. "Well," said one woman in the class, "we have these new neighbors and we took chocolate-chip cookies to them to welcome them to the neighborhood, but they never even thanked us. Is that the kind of thing we're supposed to forgive?" The discussion continued for several minutes on this superficial level.

Finally, one lady stood and said, "Look, all of that is okay. But what if something happened to you that was *really* hard to forgive? For example, suppose someone murdered a close relative, like your brother or sister? Does God expect us to forgive someone like that?" This woman had no idea that she had just told Tom's story!

Tom lost all composure at that moment. He broke down and told the class what had happened to Margie, and how he had been unable to forgive the man who had murdered her. That moment was a breakthrough in Tom's life. Later, during the worship service, he went forward and knelt at the church altar and prayed that God would give him the grace to forgive. His wife knelt with him—and so did twenty-five supportive friends from his class and from the church.

Soon afterwards, Tom—demonstrating a character of grace

that the world does not understand—tried to contact his sister's killer to express his forgiveness. The man, still in prison, refused to see him. But Tom's story doesn't end there. There was someone else who needed to hear Tom's story of grace: Esther, Margie's roommate.

Tom encountered Esther at a Christian conference in North Carolina. He hadn't seen her in years, but he recognized her from across the room and went over to speak to her. "Esther," he said, "what are you doing here?"

"My husband thought I should come," she said. "For years, I've been searching for something. I don't know what it is, but I just hurt inside all the time."

"Esther," said Tom, "are you feeling guilty over Margie's death?"

"Yes," said Esther, "as a matter of fact, I am."

"You know that what you are feeling is called 'survivor's guilt,'" said Tom. "No one blames you for what happened to Margie. It wasn't your fault. It was that man's fault."

"I know," said Esther, "but I still feel unforgiven."

"Esther," said Tom, "I want you to know that Margie and I were the closest friends any brother and sister could be. I loved her so much that the pain of losing her nearly killed me. But Esther, I forgive you."

She burst into tears, put her arms around Tom, and hugged him tightly—then she turned and went out into the night. The next morning, she looked Tom up at breakfast and said, "Tom, for years, I lived with that guilt. I was the one he wanted to kill, but Margie died in my place. I couldn't give that guilt away to anyone. I couldn't be the wife or mother I wanted to be, because I didn't have anyone who could say, 'Esther, I forgive you.' But Tom, you had the right to say it, and you said it, and your forgiveness has set me free! Tom, you've given me wings!"

That is grace to the uttermost, grace under fire, grace that absorbs this world's hostility yet responds with patience and forgiveness. That is the grace of Jesus Christ, lived out in the story of a human life. When we, like Tom, tell the Story of grace—whether through our words or through the transformed Character of our lives—we become, as the Apostle Paul says, a sweet-smelling fragrance of the grace of the Son to those around us. It is that fragrance of grace, given off by our lives, that penetrates the hearts of grace-starved people like Judith and draws them to faith in Jesus Christ.

WHAT IF ... ?

When we first encountered Judith in Barcelona, this bright, liberal television producer was angry with tract-pushing, buttonholing street evangelists. She wanted nothing to do with their religion or their Lord. She was leaning toward New Age beliefs and was completely closed to the Christian gospel.

But what if Judith were to actually *hear* the voice of grace and *feel* the touch of grace in action? How might her heart and her life be changed?

CHAPTER ELEVEN

STORY:
A Skeptic Considers

THE STORY CONTINUES: ATLANTA, JULY 1996

Darrell and Judith were still laughing.

"I know, I know," said Ben, "you guys must think I've really lost it—a confirmed agnostic like me finally 'getting religion.' But I'm serious about this. It's not just some phase I'm going through. This is *real*. And *God* is real. He's as real to me as the two of you sitting right there across the table from me! I just had to tell you. . . . Judith, what's so funny?"

"I'm not laughing at you, Ben," Judith replied. "I'm laughing at this situation. It's just so—so—" She waved her hands, reaching for words.

"What?" asked Ben.

"Incredible!" said Judith. "It's just so incredible that you would announce that you are a Christian! I mean, all the way over here, I've been trying to figure out how to explain to you two about the changes *I've* been going through in the past four years—and then, my dear old friend, you come out with *this!*"

"Wait a minute! Stop the presses!" Ben exclaimed, leaning toward her, his eyes wide. "Judith, are you saying *you've* become a Christian, too?"

"Well, no," said Judith. "That is, not exactly. I mean . . . well, maybe I ought to start at the beginning."

"Please do!" said Ben.

"The floor's all yours," added Darrell.

"Okay," she said, taking a deep breath. "Well, for me, the story starts three years ago, when I found out I was . . . pregnant."

"*Pregnant!*" Ben and Darrell chimed at once.

"Please, you two, don't interrupt me," she responded. "I want to get through this story without breaking down—and it's not going to be easy."

Darrell touched her shoulder. "Don't feel you have to—"

"No, Darrell, it's okay," she said. "I really want you both to know what's been happening in my life." She took a deep breath and forced a tight little smile before going on. "As I was saying, I found out I was pregnant. I was living with Gardner then—I told you about Gardner, didn't I?"

"That fella in the news division?"

"Yeah. Well, it was a real inconvenient time to be having a baby. My career was in full swing. Gardner was very wrapped up in his work . . . and other things. I told him about the pregnancy, and he was quiet for a long time, and then he said, 'Well, we'll have to deal with the pregnancy.' I said, 'What do you mean, deal with the pregnancy?' He said, 'Judith, you can't have a baby now.' I said, 'Why not now?' And he just sort of blurted it out, 'Because I'm seeing someone else. Another woman.'"

Judith paused for a long time. Ben and Darrell waited, not speaking. When Judith continued, a slight quaver in her voice was the only sign of the hurt that still burned inside her.

"I didn't know what to say," she said. "I had never suspected that he was seeing someone else. Never. Until that moment, I thought we were building a life together. I thought we would sit down and figure out how this baby would become a part of that life together. But Gardner was already looking for the back door to our relationship. So I asked him, 'How long have you been seeing someone else?' He said, 'A few months. I've just been waiting for the right time to tell you.' I said, 'Well, Gardner, I don't know if you've noticed, but this is not exactly the right time. In fact, your sense of timing really stinks.' Well, to make a long story short, he moved out and that was that. I sure didn't want to have his baby around as a reminder so—" She bit her lip. "So I got an abortion."

Ben's eyes glistened with compassion. "That must have been hell."

Judith shrugged. "As close to hell as I ever want to get. When he walked out on me, I just lost it. I went into an emotional tailspin. Depression, sleeplessness, crying jags, the whole nine yards. Ending the pregnancy was hard, too. I mean, politically I've always supported choice, but I used to think that abortion was for *other* women. All of a sudden, there I was in a clinic, along with a bunch of gum-popping teenagers, waiting to get my pregnancy terminated." A tear rolled down one cheek, and she dabbed at it with her napkin.

"I was depressed for the better part of a year," she continued. "I felt rejected, unlovable, lonely—I even felt guilty over the abortion. I suffered, my work suffered, the people around me suffered just to look at me. I was a total wreck.

"Then one day, while I was flipping through *USA Today*, I stopped at a beautiful full-page ad. The whole ad was about love. In fact, it was the most beautiful poetic description of love I've ever read. 'Love is patient, love is kind, love is. . . .' Well, I can't remember it all, but it ended something like, 'These three remain: faith, hope and love. But the greatest of these is love.'

"As I read those words, I realized I had never experienced that kind of love before. I wondered who wrote the ad copy, so I looked down at the bottom of the page, and there was a line of small print that said it was taken from the Bible! And it was written by the Apostle Paul! I was shocked, because I had once read a book on goddess worship and feminist theology, and that book portrayed ol' Saint Paul as the worst chauvinist since Genghis Khan! Yet those words were so beautiful! I began to wonder if that kind of love could exist in real life. So I cut out the ad and taped it next to my dresser mirror, and I read it every day before I went to work. And there was something kind of comforting in that.

"Well, about that time, I got a new boss at the network, a real nice guy named John. An older guy—fatherly, wise, kind. He became a mentor to me and gave me some great assignments. I knew John was kind of religious, and though we had a conversation about God over lunch one time, he never tried to push his beliefs on me.

"Well, I was just starting to pull out of my emotional funk and get my act together when I made a *big* mistake on the job. I mean, I really blew it big-time. I expected to get the axe for it.

"But you know what John did? He took the blame for my mistake! I mean, I've had senior producers set me up to take the blame for *their* mistakes before, but I've *never* had it work the other way around! I was totally blown away! So I asked him, 'John, why in the world did you do that?'

"He said, 'Judith, you know I'm a Christian. That means that Jesus Christ has taken the penalty for my sin upon Himself. I've received something from God called *grace*—a free gift, unmerited favor and forgiveness. From some of the things you've said over the past few weeks, I got the idea that you are someone who has not experienced much grace lately.'

"I thought, *Wow! No one* ever *said anything like that to me before!* And when John invited me to visit his church with him and his wife, I thought, *How can I say no?* So I went.

"It was a small Presbyterian church. And it was just so amazing! I mean, I thought church people would be like those street preachers out there—fanatics, preachy, telling you you're going to hell, stuff like that. But the people I met were normal—people like me! I saw an advertising exec I knew, and a model I had met on an assignment for the network. Then I heard someone call my name, and it was Karen, a friend of mine who's a lawyer with the ACLU. I said, 'What are *you* doing here?' And she said, 'I've been going to church here for two years. What are *you* doing here?'

"And that brings me right up to the present day. I'm still attending that church. I'm not saying I've become 'born again'—not yet, anyway. I'm still skeptical, I'm still Jewish, and I'm still slowly sorting it all out. But lately, a lot of what I've been hearing at church and reading in the Bible is starting to make sense. And like you, Ben,

I'm meeting with a group that studies the Bible. I've made a lot of new friends in that group. They know I'm still inquiring, that I'm not quite ready to make a commitment, yet they accept me right where I am.

"So now, Ben, old chum, you can see why I was laughing—not because I think it's weird that you're a Christian now, but because of an amazing coincidence: I'm practically a Christian myself!"

Ben was about to respond, but he was interrupted by the sound of laughter. Darrell's laughter.

"What's so funny?" Ben and Judith said in chorus.

"I can't believe it," laughed Darrell. "I just can't believe it!"

"You can't believe what?" said Ben.

Darrell put up his hand. "Just a moment. Here comes the waitress. Let's order dessert—Judith, you've just got to try the apple pie with cinnamon ice cream. Then I've got something to tell you both—and it's really gonna knock your socks off!"

PART FOUR

The Fellowship of the Holy Spirit

CHAPTER TWELVE

IN SEARCH OF POWER AND COMMUNITY

HOW DO WE REACH DARRELL?

Judith's life has been redirected by the touch of grace. When another person—her boss, a Christian television sports producer—demonstrated grace to her by taking the blame for her mistake, Judith's story collided with the Story of grace in a powerful, explosive way. This collision of stories has opened Judith's heart to a Story she was once closed to—the Story of the grace of Jesus Christ, grace that is greater than all her pain, her loneliness, and her guilt. Judith has not yet committed her life to Christ—but she is edging ever closer to the light of God's grace.

Now we turn to Darrell. How will we reach him?

Darrell is a twenty-five-year-old black attorney (and former track athlete) from South Los Angeles. He grew up poor and was raised by a devout Christian mother, but his boyhood faith crumbled under the traumatic loss of his mother due to cancer. Darrell looks back on the religion of his childhood with a bit of wistfulness. He longs for those days when he believed in God, when he believed there really was Someone who listened when he prayed, Someone who answered and acted, Someone who was *real*. But as an adult, having been deeply disappointed by the religion of his childhood, he feels there is nothing to believe in anymore.

How do we reach someone like Darrell?

A GENERATION IN SEARCH OF EMPOWERMENT

As nations and as individuals, our world is searching for something—for a purpose, for a cause, for empowerment. People no longer feel in control of their destinies, their lives, or their world. Our cities simmer—and sometimes burn—with outrage and frustration. Our political institutions are impotent. The church seems too insignificant—or even irrelevant—to make a difference.

Even though our postmodern generation has lost faith in the power of God, people are still hungry for personal empowerment, a sense that their lives are under control, and inner direction. That is why various interest groups—from labor unions to racial minorities to radical feminists to political lobbies to the religious right to the religious left—seek political empowerment. That is why motivational gurus such as Anthony Robbins sell millions of dollars worth of books and tapes with titles like *Unlimited Power* and *Awaken the Giant Within*. That is why thousands of people pay enormous sums of money to hear actress/seminar speaker Shirley MacLaine tell them, "You are God." People hunger for power— power over their own lives, their own destinies, their own problems.

The Story we have to share with this generation is the Story of a God who comes to them as an empowering Presence. It is the Story of Acts 1:8—"You will receive power when the Holy Spirit comes on you." It is the Story of Ephesians 3:20—"Now to him who is able to do immeasurably more than all we ask or imagine, according to his power that is at work within us." It is the Story of more power than was ever envisioned by any motivational pitchman or New Age guru.

A GENERATION IN SEARCH OF COMMUNITY

But postmodern people are not only hungry for empowerment. They are also hungry for *community*, for a sense of fellowship with

Someone or Something larger than themselves. Although most people are not aware of it, what they *really* hunger for is *fellowship with God*. As the psalmist wrote,

> My soul thirsts for you,
>   my body longs for you,
> in a dry and weary land
>   where there is no water.[1]

We were all born with a desire for intimacy with our Creator, even though many people try to fulfill that desire with lesser things.

Consider, then, this outrageous possibility: Do we dare to believe that we, as followers of Jesus Christ, could be *empowered* by God to begin a movement toward national conversion? And do we dare to believe that we could be used by God to stake out a new *community* for Him in this postmodern world, a community bonded together by the *fellowship* of the Holy Spirit?

That *would* be a paradigm shift, wouldn't it!

We tend to see the world and its problems as a huge circle, and the church of Jesus Christ as a dot somewhere on the edge of that circle. We tend to see ourselves as dispossessed by our times. But God wants us to see His plan as *huge* and *unstoppable* and *irresistible*—and the world as a small part of the great, cosmic purpose of God.

The early Church did not suffer the "inferiority complex" we often feel today. Though despised and persecuted, the early Church refused to accept the world's devalued assessment. The first-century Christians believed in a big God—and empowered by His Spirit, they turned the world upside down. We need to recapture that vision. We need to see the enormity of the gospel as it looms over our world.

A young Japanese pastor came to me following Singapore '87, a Lausanne conference for younger leaders, and said, "I've gone through a paradigm shift. Before this conference, I saw my church as being in the world. Now I see the world in which God has placed my church."

That is the vision we all need to see. And when we glimpse

this vision of the empowering, irresistible "bigness" of God the Holy Spirit—God the Evangelist, God who has come among us as an empowering, fellowshiping Presence—then we will see people like Darrell respond to our story. Why? Because Darrell and people like him are hungry for empowerment, for fellowship, and for the reality of God's presence. They long to hear the Story we have to share with them: the Story of the fellowship of the Holy Spirit.

OUR STORY: THE FELLOWSHIP OF THE HOLY SPIRIT

In his book *Christianity Rediscovered*, Vincent Donovan shares an incident from his own experience that makes a powerful point. Donovan is an Irish Catholic missionary who ministered among the Masai people of East Africa. He went to the Masai with his Catholic evangelization background and he made two discoveries: (1) that his traditional evangelization methods would not work with the Masai people; and (2) that the Jesus he was presenting was not a Jesus that the Masai people could relate to. He realized he had to go back and rediscover Jesus all over again. So Donovan was driven back to the Scriptures, and there he discovered some fascinating truths that transformed his own life and faith.

One important discovery Donovan made was *the crucial importance of community*. He learned that the Masai clans and tribes had as much unique personality as an individual person does. He learned that he had to deal with the Masai on their own collective terms. Because of the way the Masai culture functioned, he could not go from individual to individual and make converts one by one. He had to share the gospel with the entire clan, then let the clan decide if it would follow Christ or not. (We'll set aside for the moment the prickly question of just how valid mass, community conversions are, and how they relate to an individual new birth.)

For about a year, Vincent Donovan taught these people everything he knew about Jesus. Then at the end of that year, he gathered them all together and said (through his interpreter, the chief), "Now I've told you the gospel. It's up to you to decide. You can accept or reject Jesus as your Lord, and if you decide to accept Him, I will perform a ceremony of public baptism.

"I'm going to go away for a week. While I'm gone, I want you to think about it and discuss it, and when I return, you may tell me what you have decided. But if the clan does decide to convert to Christianity, there will be some exceptions made. For example, this old man here will not be baptized because he's been out herding cattle too much and he hasn't heard enough of the gospel to make an informed decision. But that woman there has been very faithful, so she'll be baptized. Those two young warriors have been gone too much, and that woman is lazy; they can't be baptized. That person is attentive; he may be baptized. That person is stupid; no baptism for him."

He continued like this, going from person to person around the clan, dividing them up, deciding who would and would not be baptized. The old chief stopped him and said, "Padre, why are you trying to separate us? During this year that you've been teaching us, even when you weren't here, we've sat around the fire at night and talked about the things you've told us. Yes, there are lazy ones in this community, but they've been helped by the energetic ones. Yes, there are stupid ones in this community, but they've been helped by those who are intelligent. Yes, there are some with little faith in this village, but they've been helped by those with much faith. Would you turn and drive out the lazy ones, the stupid ones, and the ones with little faith? Don't they need Jesus, too? From the first day you came, we have been talking about the things you have told us, and now, after a year, I want to tell you: Padre, *we* believe."

Donovan later observed that he had never heard the words "*we* believe" spoken with such intensity and conviction before. Donovan was very impressed, so he said to them, "If you decide to follow Jesus, what will you call yourselves?"

They talked for quite a while among themselves, and then the chief spoke up again. "Our name," he said, "will be the *Orporor Longai*—the Age-Group Brotherhood of God."

Among the Masai, the *orporor* was a seven-year time span. Every male initiated into manhood during a given *orporor* belongs to the brotherhood of that seven-year order. The wives of these brothers also are considered part of the order. The sense of belonging and community conveyed by this brotherhood was the most sacred notion in their culture. That is why they selected this concept as their word for "church." In making this decision, they also redefined the concept of *orporor*. No longer would an *orporor* represent a single tribe for a single span of seven years, but it would henceforth extend until the end of time, and would encompass *all* tribes, *all* clans, *all* genders, *all* nationalities. It would be the first universal brotherhood of Masai people.

If you and I were to walk into the midst of an *Orporor Longai* worship service, we might not recognize it as a church. "Where's the sanctuary?" we might say. "Where are the hymnals? Where's the Sunday school? Where's the fellowship hall?" Yet, if a first-century Christian walked into many of our churches today, he might say, "This is a church? Where is the deep sense of community, the bondedness of believers? Where is the empowering presence of the Holy Spirit?"

As he groped to find a way to express Christ in terms that were comprehensible to the Masai mind, and then as he watched these Masai people create their own church, using the conceptual building blocks of their own culture, Vincent Donovan rediscovered Christianity. He saw the clear, clean simplicity of Christian truth as it was distilled into this new Masai church-brotherhood. And, he reflected, there was no danger that these Masai people would ever fall into the trap we Western Christians so easily slip into: the trap of confusing the *church* with a *building*. These tribespeople properly understood that the church is a brotherhood, a community— a fellowship of the Holy Spirit.

Where is the fellowship of the Holy Spirit in our postmodern world? Where is the community of spiritual empowerment that is going to fill the void within our friend Darrell? Where do we point people who are searching for a sense of belonging and spiritual reality?

The answer, once again, is to be found in the simple pattern of narrative evangelism: *The Story produces a Vision, and the Vision transforms Character.*

We have seen the Story of the love of God the Father as it sweeps throughout the Scriptures, and most specifically as it is distilled in the story of the loving father and his prodigal son. We have seen the Story of the grace of Jesus Christ, the Story of the God who gave up everything He had in Heaven in order to take the form of a servant, to offer His life for ours, to give us forgiveness and eternal life beyond our ability to earn or deserve.

But what is the Story of the Holy Spirit? And what is the Vision this Story produces? And what is the transformed Character that emerges from that Vision?

The Story of God the Holy Spirit is the Story we find in the book of Acts. There we see the infant church—that first-century fellowship of believers—receiving a Gift. It is a Gift that God the Father has entrusted to the risen Lord, who in turn pours it out upon those early believers. "You *will* receive power!" says the resurrected Jesus. "You *will* be my witnesses! You *will* receive the gift of the Holy Spirit!" It is not a command that Jesus gives to the early Church. It is a *promise:* "You *will* receive."

Then we see God go to work. And we discover that He is an all-powerful God who works through a minority strategy. His strength is perfected in human weakness. The God of the early Church of Acts is the same God who worked through Gideon's tiny band of 300 commandos, because his first army of 32,000 soldiers, and then 10,000, were *too many* to win the battle against the Midianites! The God of Acts is a God who doesn't despise broken reeds and smoking flax. He is a God who places his treasure in common clay pots. Acts is the Story of a weak, outnumbered, persecuted church— but it is a church in action, a church on the move, because God's empowering Presence, the Spirit, is poured out upon it.

That Story—the Story of the empowering Presence, the restless, roving, energizing Spirit—is the story of transformed lives. In the book of Acts, we see the Story of God colliding with the stories of individual people, one after another. In each of those stories, *transformation* takes place. *Conversion* takes place. The Story of God calls the stories of men and women into question again and again in the book of Acts, prompting them to say, "Perhaps my story isn't the whole story!" Then they become caught up in the Story of Jesus.

Before Saul collided with Jesus on the road to Damascus, he first collided with Stephen, giving assent as Stephen was being stoned to death for his witness. Though Saul didn't experience conversion until years after watching the courageous, faithful death of Stephen, it is clear that the story of Stephen's life impacted the story of Saul. It may have been a latent impact, like a bomb with a delayed-action fuse, but the Story of Jesus, lived out in the martyr's death of Stephen, must have played an explosive part in shaping the Vision and Character of the man who would later become the Apostle Paul.

It is a pattern we see again and again throughout Acts. The Ethiopian eunuch collides with Philip. Cornelius collides with Peter. Apollos collides with Priscilla and Aquila. King Agrippa collides with Paul. And all of them collide with the Spirit of Jesus. Throughout the book of Acts we see communities of Jesus being planted—little bands of brothers and sisters that spring up from Jerusalem to Asia Minor to Rome to Spain. Their numbers increase, and a new quality of life emerges. No, these are not idyllic, utopian communities. They sin and squabble, they experience ethnic rivalries. But in spite of all that, the Spirit of Jesus, the character of Jesus, is forming within them.

These early Christian communities were *suffering* communities—standing against a hostile world and *rejoicing* when they had the privilege of suffering for the name of Jesus. They were dragged out of their homes, beaten and imprisoned, stoned to death and burned alive—yet they did not whine or complain about being "victims." How different from the mind-set we Christians have today! Sure, we face hostility and criticism, we get a bad press sometimes, but no one stones us or drags us from our families because of our faith. Yet we are so quick to assume the victim role: "Did you hear what that comedian said about Christians on 'Jay Leno' last night? Did you see how Christians were caricatured in that *Newsweek* article? Did you see that unfavorable piece about churches on CNN last week? Oh, Lord, your people are being martyred in the media! How much more of this persecution do we have to take?!"

The role of victim is not a biblical role. We may be martyrs, we may even be called upon one day to lay down our lives for the sake of our Lord—but we are *never* victims. The Bible never counsels us to wallow in self-pity when we are persecuted. Rather, the Bible tells us we are to *rejoice* and count ourselves as *blessed* when we suffer for the name of Jesus.

In the book of Acts we also see God the Holy Spirit in His role as the master strategist. I would encourage you to sit down and read through the book of Acts in a single sitting. You'll see that this is not the story of evangelists and church leaders sitting down to develop grand strategies. No human being or committee of human beings could have planned the amazing course of events that we see in this book. Rather, what we see is the Story of the sovereign Spirit closing this door and opening that door, while the early Christians say, "Look what God the Evangelist is doing! How are we going to be part of this?"

And that Story becomes the Vision of the early Church.

OUR VISION: A VISION OF POWER

The Story of Acts is a Vision of human beings in intimate fellowship and partnership with the God who created the universe. This Vision gives us an expanded understanding of God, and of the role God has for each of us. Instead of focusing on our limitations, we are now free to focus on what God *can* do and what he *wants* to do through each of us.

As the restless, roving Spirit moved in the church of Acts, He gave them the Vision that became their motivation. That Vision began with the Great Commission: "All authority in heaven and on earth has been given to me. Therefore go and make disciples."[2] Yet the Great Commission alone does not explain the dynamic courage, faith, and effectiveness of those early believers as they extended the reach of the gospel Story. For when Jesus commissioned them, He not only said "Go." He also said "Wait."

"Do not leave Jerusalem," Jesus said in the opening verses of Acts, "but *wait* for the gift my Father promised."[3] When the disciples received the poured-out gift of the Holy Spirit, the Great Commission that Jesus had given them was filled with *power*.

And young men saw *visions*.

And old men dreamed *dreams*.

And that restless Spirit expanded frontiers and broke down barriers.

Ironically, the first barrier that needed to be broken down was within the minds of the disciples themselves. It was a barrier of prejudice. These early Christians had heard Jesus say, "When you go to be my witnesses, you must start at Jerusalem, then go to Judea and Samaria and to the uttermost parts of the earth."[4] But what Jesus said and what the early Christians *thought* He said were two different things. They heard the words of Jesus through the filter of their ethnic prejudice. They *thought* He said, "You shall be My witnesses to the *Jews* in Jerusalem, to the *Jews* in Judea, to the *Jews* in Samaria, and to the *Jews* in the uttermost parts of the earth." They didn't understand that the fellowship of the Holy Spirit was about to extend to the Gentiles as well as the Jews. That was the barrier in their minds.

How did God shatter this barrier? With a Vision.

One of the most prejudiced and tradition-bound members of this early fellowship was that famous witnessing Christian named Peter. One night, as he lay sleeping on a roof, Peter had a vision of a sheet let down from Heaven, filled with nonkosher animals. And the voice of God called to him, "Get up and eat, Peter." But Peter refused to eat, because the meat was nonkosher—that is, "unclean." But the voice of God insisted, "What I have cleansed, don't you call 'unclean.'"

That Vision shattered Peter's prejudice. He realized that the focus of this Vision was not meat, but people—those "nonkosher" Gentiles Peter had always snubbed and avoided. God was telling Peter that His Kingdom was throwing its doors wide open, to receive not only the Jews but also non-Jews. Henceforth, there would be no class of people whom Christians could write off as "unclean." God loves Jews and Gentiles, Republicans and Democrats, rich and poor, young and old, boomers and busters, Anglos and African-Americans, Asians and Hispanics, liberals and conservatives, people with leprosy, people with AIDS, people married with children, divorced people, single people—and He wants to bring all these different kinds of people together into one big joyous fellowship of the Holy Spirit. All of this amazing truth is embedded in Peter's rooftop vision—and this truth is just as powerful and convicting today as it was in Peter's day.

OUR CHARACTER: HUMILITY AND VULNERABILITY

The Story produces a Vision, and the Vision transforms Character.

How was Peter's Character transformed by his rooftop vision? Instantly, his supercilious bias against Gentiles was replaced by an obedient, humble spirit. He experienced a radical reversal of everything that was culturally and religiously ingrained in him. The restless, roving Spirit of God sent Peter to Cornelius, a Gentile army officer.

It is important to note what Peter says to him. Many of us, when we witness to others, take the position, "I have the truth and you need to hear it." But Peter assumes a posture of humility and expresses himself in a vulnerable way. He does not say, "Cornelius, this is what *you* need to hear." No, the first words out of Peter's mouth are, "This is what God has shown *me*."[5]

Here, Peter gives us a powerful lesson in authentic evangelism. He shows us one of the most important differences between genuine witnessing and mere proselytizing.

Proselytizing is the sawed-off shotgun approach to evangelism: You load up with scattershot ammunition, aim at anything that moves, and blast away! "Hey, you filthy sinners! You're going to hell if you don't repent! Yeah, go on, ignore me, walk on by, but you'll be sorry! Someday, when it's too late, you'll remember I tried to warn you!" Proselytizers don't care about affecting human hearts, about listening to human needs, about healing human hurts. Proselytizers just shoot their message at people in hopes of somehow hitting a vital spot and making a convert. If nobody listens, that's fine, it just confirms their smug assessment of those unclean heathen.

But Peter is no mere proselytizer. He's an authentic evangelist. He doesn't go to Cornelius and call him unclean. Instead, he levels the playing field between himself and Cornelius. He says, "I'm no more special or holy or intelligent than anybody else. I'm just a guy like you. And Cornelius, I just want to share with you what God, in His grace, has shown me."[6] Proselytizers seek to convert others to their point of view. Authentic evangelists, however, are open to allowing God to *change them* as they humbly, prayerfully carry the life-changing Story of Jesus to others.

The Vision of Jesus that Paul received on the Damascus road transformed his Character and drove him for the rest of his life. Is there a Vision driving your life right now? Are you open to the completely new direction God wants to take you for the rest of your life? Are you willing to allow Him to invade your life and transform your Character as He invaded and transformed the life of Paul?

Peter had a Vision of the church, a fellowship of the Holy Spirit where no person, Jew or Gentile, would be considered unclean. That Vision not only transformed Peter's character, but it also transformed the character of the early Church. To which "Cornelius"— to which unreached, unlikely, "unclean" person—is God the Holy Spirit sending you right now? What is the barrier that prevents you from seeing this person as God sees him or her? Can you envision the "ripple effect" that would radiate out to others from the transformed life of this "unclean" person, once he or she has been made "clean" by Jesus Christ?

I urge you: *Pray for Vision.*

Pray that God would not only use you as His instrument to change others, but that you, too, would be transformed by the Story you tell. Pray that the same restless, roving Presence who was poured out upon the church of Acts would be poured out upon you. Ask God for the grace to dream dreams and see a new Vision. Pray that God would use this Vision to transform your Character and make you His witness, His evangelist.

THREE STEPS TO A NEW VISION

Whenever I can, I ask people—particularly young men and women—"What is your Vision?" If they say, "I don't have a Vision," I answer, "Well, if you *did* have a Vision, what would it be? And if you can't envision a Vision, what do you dream?" They usually say, "Well, how do I get a Vision?" My answer: "God gives it. But don't expect Him to give you a Vision as you passively wait. Actively *pray* for Vision. Actively *seek* a Vision from His Spirit."

And how do you actively seek God's Vision for your life? Let me suggest to you a practical three-step process:

1. Observe.
2. Reflect.
3. Act.

First, *observe* what is happening in the world with your eyes wide open. What are people thinking and doing? What are the trends, events, and influences that shape the thinking of the people around you? What are their needs and desires? What is God doing in the world? Observe constantly and prayerfully. Keep your eyes trained on the radar screen of your soul until God begins to point you in a direction or toward a person, a "Cornelius," who needs to see and hear the Story God has entrusted to you.

Then, *reflect* on what you observe. Think about it. Talk about it. Pray about it. Journal about it. Write about it. Reflect on it again and again, from every conceivable angle. Study the Scriptures and seek out what God is trying to say to you about reaching your neighbor, your brother-in-law, your sister, your roommate, your coworker, your workplace, your urban world, your campus, the Asian refugee community in your city, the black or Hispanic community in your city, the Masai in Africa—whomever God is giving you a Vision to reach.

Then *act*—even if, at first, you only have the courage to act in a small way. *Act* in obedience to the Vision. Act on the Vision God has given to you.

When God's Vision becomes our vision, our character is transformed. Then, God can move us out into our neighborhood, our marketplace, and our world, and He can make us His storytellers.

CHAPTER THIRTEEN

THE "FIVE-FINGER EXERCISE"

THE FINGER OF GOD

The book of Acts is a record not so much of the acts of people, nor the acts of the church, but rather of the *acts of the Holy Spirit*. In that book we see the Spirit giving power to people and drawing them together into fellowships, redeeming communities, which quickly spread throughout Palestine and Asia Minor and across the Roman world. These communities were . . .

- Transformed by the Holy Spirit
- Empowered by the Holy Spirit
- Gripped by the Holy Spirit
- Guided by the Holy Spirit
- Gifted by the Holy Spirit
- United by the Holy Spirit

As we look closely at these various *acts of the Holy Spirit*, we begin to notice a fascinating truth about the Spirit of God: He is very active, very involved, very much at work in our world.

In Luke 11, we see a vivid illustration of the action of the Spirit. There, Jesus drives a demon out of a deaf-mute man, then says He has driven out this demon "by the *finger* of God."[1] In the parallel passage in Matthew 12, Jesus says He has driven out this demon "by the *Spirit* of God."[2] Clearly then, the *Spirit* of God is in some sense also the *finger* of God—an image that suggests that the Spirit of God is active, performing the work of God.

We can picture the activity of the Holy Spirit in terms of a "five-finger exercise." What do fingers do? Among other things, fingers can . . .

- Write
- Grip
- Point
- Touch
- Beckon

As we will see, there is a sense in which the "finger of God," the Spirit of God, can perform all of these actions, too.

Finger 1: The Beckoning Finger

We beckon with our fingers—and so does God. The Holy Spirit is the beckoning finger of God, creating a holy dissatisfaction, a holy restlessness, a holy desire for union with Him. The Spirit beckons in three ways: He *convicts*, He *converts*, and He *conveys*. Let's examine each of these functions of the beckoning finger of God.

The Holy Spirit convicts. In Acts 2, Peter preaches to the people on the day of Pentecost. The Holy Spirit pricks the hearts of the people and they respond: "What shall we do?"[3] Dwight L. Moody described that event this way: "Peter lifted up Jesus and the Holy Spirit said, 'Amen!'" The people were cut to the heart, convicted of their need by the beckoning finger of God.

The Holy Spirit converts. In Acts 11, we see the Holy Spirit— pictured as "the Lord's hand"—turning a great number of people to the Lord, converting them from what they once were to what

God wants them to be in Christ: "The Lord's hand was with them, and a great number of people believed and turned to the Lord."[4]

The Holy Spirit conveys power. In Acts 2, we see the double gift of the Holy Spirit and the risen Lord—*pardon* and *power*—as Peter says, "Repent and be baptized, every one of you, in the name of Jesus Christ for the forgiveness of your sins [that's *pardon*]. And you will receive the gift of the Holy Spirit [that's *power*]."[5]

Once we recognize that beckoning is not our job, but the work of the Spirit, we can relax and tell our Story. Our task as Christian witnesses is not to *create* a hunger for God, but to *uncover* the hunger God has already placed there. And how do we uncover the spiritual hunger in the people around us? By acting as an "aroma" of Christ, announcing that the Bread of Life has come.

Walk into a house where bread is baking, and you don't even have to travel to the kitchen to catch the aroma. The fragrance of baking bread fills the whole house. It stirs the taste buds and sends a message to the brain: "There is fresh, hot, wholesome bread baking here!" In the same way, you and I can act as the aroma of Jesus, the Bread of Life. If the way we live our lives gives off the scent of Christ, then people will come to us, drinking in the aroma of our lives, wanting to know where this Bread they have detected can be found.

Socrates once said, "The best sauce for food is hunger." Food never tastes better than when we are famished, when our need for food is great. And the things of God never taste better than when hungry, famished, starving people recognize their great need of Him. We teach truth, we model light, we expose darkness, we pray, we trust, we believe—and as people around us watch our lives, they recognize their own need. They hunger for what we have. Jesus said we are salt, imparting a savor of Himself that the hungry people around us crave to experience.[6] And the Apostle Paul pictured us as a tantalizing aroma of Jesus Christ.[7]

Our postmodern generation is a hungry generation—hungry for fellowship, hungry for empowerment, hungry for God Himself. Though the people around us sense their hunger and neediness, they often fail to understand what they are *truly* hungry for. So they gorge themselves on empty, worthless things that dull the hunger pangs but do not truly satisfy: alcohol, drugs, materialism, success, entertainment, promiscuous sex, gambling, and addictive relationships.

Fifty years ago, an Episcopalian clergyman named Sam Shoemaker understood this principle as he worked with alcoholics in New York City. He properly diagnosed the self-destructive disorder that gripped these addicted people. They were hungry for God, but they were stuffing their hunger with alcohol. So, together with a man named Bill Wilson, Shoemaker helped to formulate the twelve steps of Alcoholics Anonymous (AA). In those steps, alcoholics acknowledge their powerlessness over their addictions, commit themselves to the care of God, and live their lives in daily reliance upon God through prayer and meditation. In all the years since the founding of AA, no treatment for alcoholism or other addictions has ever been as effective as the twelve steps. Why? Because the twelve steps correctly diagnose and treat the underlying cause of addiction: a hunger for God. A friend of mine, who has been in AA for years, calls it a "program of attraction." It attracts people whose hunger for God has been uncovered by the intense need and the intense pain of their addiction.

My friend Ford Madison is a businessman and for many years was a member of my board. Thirty years ago, he was working in the Nicaraguan branch office of a large American dairy corporation. Ford had a man working in his office, a Nicaraguan named Reynaldo, whom he described as "one of the most delightful and unreliable men I've ever known." Reynaldo was a thoroughly charming fellow but an unproductive worker, so—regretfully— Ford had to let him go.

Then in 1991, Ford had an occasion to return to Nicaragua, and while there he asked around and finally located this man, Reynaldo. When they met, Reynaldo said, "I remember you. You're the man who used to exercise and pray every morning."

"Can I buy you a drink?" asked Ford.

Reynaldo agreed, and they went to a restaurant, ordered something to drink, and began to talk. They reminisced for a few minutes, then Ford said, "Reynaldo, I want to give you two things. First, I want to give you this." He reached into his pocket and pulled out a gold pin in the form of a cross. "I want you to have this as a token of friendship between us."

"Thank you very much," said Reynaldo, taking the pin and turning it over in his hands.

"The other thing I want to give you," Ford continued, "is something I *can't* give you."

Reynaldo looked at him quizzically.

"Only God can give you this thing," said Ford. "It's the gift of eternal life." He reached into his pocket again and this time he pulled out a booklet, *Steps to Peace with God*, and he handed the booklet to Reynaldo. "This book tells how you can have eternal life," he added. "I'd like to talk to you about that."

Reynaldo looked at the book, then put it down on the table. "I'm hungry. Let's eat now, talk later."

Ford called the waiter back and they ordered lunch. They ate, and when they had finished eating, Reynaldo picked up the book again and said, "Okay. Now, show me."

So Ford took him through the booklet, and right there at that restaurant table Reynaldo prayed and gave his life to Jesus Christ. Today, he's involved in a church and a Bible study in Nicaragua. "Thirty years ago," Ford Madison reflects, "Reynaldo wouldn't have given me the time of day. I just wouldn't have been able to reach him. He was too busy chasing women and having a good time. He had no awareness of any spiritual hunger inside. But a lot of things had happened in his life these past thirty years. I think the catalyst was probably the death of a close friend due to cancer." It took Reynaldo thirty years to become aware of his hunger— but when the time was right, the Holy Spirit, the finger of God, beckoned to Reynaldo, and Reynaldo eagerly responded.

The Spirit beckons to people all around us, every day. The Spirit makes them aware of their need and their hunger. Our task is to meet them at their point of need and feed their hunger with the Bread of Life, the only food that satisfies.

Finger 2: The Writing Finger

You may have felt frustrated by programed approaches to evangelism. If so, you are not alone. You can find more "how to" programs in North America than in any other place in the world, including programs on "how to be an evangelist." You can also find more *frustration* with "how to" programs here than any other place— including many *good* programs. I believe that "programed" approaches to evangelism are part of our problem.

The Holy Spirit, the writing finger of God, *deprograms* evangelism. I'm not saying that we don't need good programs. But the Holy Spirit can take whatever effort we offer Him, including our programs, and transform them into something much *more* than programed approaches—something living, dynamic, and transforming. True evangelism must grow out of who we authentically are and who God authentically is. How does the Holy Spirit deprogram our witnessing and make us more authentic storytellers of His Story?

By writing His Story on our lives.

We use our fingers to write, and God uses His finger, the Holy Spirit, to write as well. God has written His personality into the stars. The psalmist wrote:

> When I consider your heavens,
>   the work of your fingers, . . .
> what is man that you are mindful of him?[8]

And in the book of Exodus, we see that God wrote His law, the Ten Commandments, on tablets of stone.[9]

But perhaps the most amazing writing God the Spirit has ever done was when He wrote Christ upon our lives: "You are a letter from Christ . . . written not with ink but with the Spirit of the living God, not on tablets of stone but on tablets of human hearts."[10] The Spirit writes the *love* of Jesus, the *joy* of Jesus, and the *authenticity* of Jesus upon our lives. Witnessing does not mean putting on a spiritual front. Witnessing means being honest about who and what we are. The writing finger of God, writing the Story of Jesus across the lives of His people, makes evangelism *authentic*—and makes God *real* to the people around us.

Our son Sandy died during heart surgery at the age of twenty-one. The cardiologist who took care of him—Dr. John Gallagher, a world-renowned electrophysiological cardiologist—was stunned by Sandy's death. He was stunned for two reasons: (1) because he was confident that, despite the seriousness of Sandy's heart condition, he was young enough and strong enough to survive the surgery; and (2) because he had gotten to know Sandy. The courage and resilient faith of our son Sandy had an impact on Dr. Gallagher's life that I didn't learn about until several years later.

On the tenth anniversary of the founding of the Sandy Ford Memorial Fund, we invited Dr. Gallagher to speak to a group of fund supporters. During his talk, Dr. Gallagher made a surprise revelation. "I was very bright, very competent, very confident as a physician," he said, "but when I encountered Sandy Ford, I learned just how much I didn't know. Facing the risks of open-heart surgery, this young man had a courage and a peace that I wished I had. I saw something in Sandy Ford's eyes that reminded me that there was something more to life than I was experiencing. I was the doctor, he was my patient, but he had a hand in my healing. Two years ago, during a dark period in my life—in large part because of the impact of this young man on my life—I found Sandy's Lord."

The writing finger of God had written His Story on Sandy's life before he died. Sandy's doctor read that Story, and his life was changed.

What is the Story God is writing in your life today?

Finger 3: The Gripping Finger
You may have felt inhibited and intimidated at the prospect of opening your mouth and telling the Story of God to another person: "What will I say? What will this person think? What if I get tongue-tied? What if I say the wrong thing? What if I say something that drives this person further away from God instead of attracting the person to God?" These are common fears among those who want to share their faith. The key to overcoming these fears is to understand and appropriate the power of the *gripping finger* of God.

The issue is one of *confidence*. If we lack confidence that God will be with us when we witness, then we will lack boldness as we speak. If we lack boldness, we will be silent. If we are silent, the Story will go untold. And that is the tragedy that takes place in the life of Christian after Christian. In fact, lack of confidence is the number-one problem that Christians face in witnessing to others.

Surveys have shown that very few Christians—somewhere between 5 and 10 percent—have ever shared their faith with another person and prayed with that person as he makes a commitment to Christ. Clearly, the 90 to 95 percent who have never led someone to the Lord are missing out on one of the greatest thrills of the Christian life! These people represent a huge mass of untapped evangelistic energy in the church. If only this great "silent majority" of the church could overcome its fear and become emboldened to move out and tell the Story. Just think of the impact the church would have if each of these silent Christians would share the Story with just one other person within her or his sphere of influence.

It could happen—if this "silent majority" could acquire the confidence that comes through reliance upon the *gripping finger* of God, the Holy Spirit.

It is perfectly normal to experience a certain amount of fear when we witness. There is fear of the unknown. Fear of change. Fear of rejection. Fear of making ourselves vulnerable. Yet, whatever our fears, however well-founded they may be, few of us have to face the level of fear that must have been an ever-present companion of the Apostle Paul: Fear of beatings. Fear of stonings. Fear of riots. Fear of imprisonment. Fear of floggings. Yet Paul persevered in his witness, amid all these dangers and more. Why?

He had confidence in the gripping finger of God, the Holy Spirit. And what was the confidence of Paul? He tells us in Romans 8:16—the Holy Spirit *assures*. "The Spirit himself testifies with our spirit that we are God's children." He tells us in Ephesians 1:13—the Holy Spirit *seals*. "Having believed, you were marked in [Christ] with a seal, the promised Holy Spirit." He tells us in Ephesians 3:16—the Holy Spirit *strengthens*. "I pray that out of his glorious riches he may strengthen you with power through his Spirit in your inner being."

Imagine the fear Ananias faced before he went to see Saul! What gave him the boldness to do as God told him? Confidence in the Spirit of God. And what gave Peter the boldness to go to

Cornelius, even though doing so went against everything he had been taught about Gentiles ever since he was a child? Confidence in the Spirit of God. And what gave Philip the boldness to go and share the Story of God with the Ethiopian treasurer? Confidence in the Spirit of God.

The gripping finger of God holds us securely, giving us the strength and assurance to face our fears—even to face a hostile world—and boldly tell our Story.

Finger 4: The Pointing Finger
The pointing finger of God speaks of the guidance of the Holy Spirit. Many of us are confused at the prospect of witnessing to others. We dither uncertainly between two prevailing attitudes toward evangelism:

- Attitude 1: "We've always done it this way!" That's the viewpoint of the church-as-mausoleum crowd.
- Attitude 2: "We've never tried this before! Let's do it!" That's the viewpoint of the anything-goes proponents, the church-as-silly-putty crowd.

The pointing finger of God gives us wisdom, guiding our evangelistic choices. Sometimes the old approaches are the most effective, sometimes a new approach is required. The Holy Spirit enables us to know what is the best response to each evangelistic opportunity.

John Wesley once said, "In evangelism, we should second the motions of the Holy Spirit." When the Spirit says "I move," our job is to second that motion. Where is God working? What doors is He opening? What doors is He closing? Where do we find responsive hearts? The Spirit knows, and He reveals His answers to us day by day, step by step, decision by decision.

We see the pointing finger of God again and again in the book of Acts. In Acts 8, the Spirit pointed Philip to the Ethiopian eunuch. In Acts 9, He pointed Ananias to Saul. In Acts 10, He pointed Peter to Cornelius. In Acts 13, He moved Paul and his missionary companions to cross the cultural barrier and carry the gospel Story to the Gentiles. That is the pattern of activity of the pointing finger of

God. When we reach a crossroads and do not know which road to take, the Spirit is there, giving wisdom and insight, pointing us along the path of God's own choosing.

But what about *planning?* Does the pointing finger of God permit us to plan and strategize our witnessing efforts? How does our planning relate to the Spirit's leading?

Study carefully the pattern in the book of Acts and you will see that all of Acts is a response to God's initiative. God is the master strategist and the primary actor in evangelism. God was in charge, and the grand strategy was all His. He was the door-opener and the door-closer. The job of those early believers was to simply look for the open doors and walk through them. They didn't waste time on closed doors. They prayed for closed doors to open, but they didn't try to batter those closed doors down by human force.

Whenever a closed door was suddenly flung open by the Holy Spirit, the early Christians became a rapid response force. They consistently and aggressively took advantage of every opportunity. When God made the grand strategy clear, they used whatever tactics would be effective to tell the Story of God to the world.

Throughout the book of Acts, we see the Spirit of God, the pointing finger, acting and leading by a combination of factors. He used *negative* factors (persecution, opposition, closed doors) and *positive* factors (such as Paul's vision of the man from Macedonia calling him to his country). He used *personal* factors (the private vision experiences of Paul and Peter) and corporate factors (*"we* sought to go"). He used *intuitive* factors (inner guidance within the soul of a leader such as Paul) and *rational* factors (data gathering, discussion, and logical debate).

Is there a role for human planning in God's strategy of evangelism? Yes! But we must define our terms. The kind of planning that fits the pattern of Acts, and that is responsive to the pointing finger of God, is planning that I would define as "acting thoughtfully in response to God's initiatives." The Holy Spirit gives us discernment as we make our plans. As Paul writes in Ephesians 5:15-17, we are to live carefully, not as unwise, but as wise. We are to make the most of every opportunity, seeking always to understand the Lord's will, seeking always to be filled with the guiding

Spirit of God. The Holy Spirit enables us to take off our blinders of self-will and self-deception, so that we can focus on reality. He enables us to lay plans that interlock with His grand strategy.

Finger 5: The Liberating Finger

The liberating finger of God touches us, setting us free to tell our Story. "Now the Lord is the Spirit," writes Paul, "and where the Spirit of the Lord is, there is freedom."[11] You are not God's robot or God's puppet in the world, acting out a predetermined program whenever He pushes your buttons or pulls your strings. You are God's agent in the world, and he has deployed you, giving you the freedom to choose a course, to make decisions, to act creatively and independently, while operating within His overall design and strategy.

We see the liberating finger of God in action throughout the Bible, beginning in the Old Testament. In Exodus 31, God affirms the calling of a man named Bezalel to a ministry in the arts—an affirmation of the fact that there are many ways in which we can minister for God and tell His Story. In this passage, God says to Moses, "See, I have chosen Bezalel son of Uri, the son of Hur, of the tribe of Judah, and I have filled him with the Spirit of God, with skill, ability and knowledge in all kinds of crafts—to make artistic designs for work in gold, silver and bronze, to cut and set stones, to work in wood, and to engage in all kinds of craftsmanship."[12]

We see the liberating finger of God in action throughout the New Testament. In Luke 11, Jesus liberated a man from demonic oppression by the liberating finger of God. That same Holy Spirit is at work today, liberating men and women from oppression, sin, and addictions, so that they can fulfill their potential in Christ. He has written the Story of Jesus upon our lives, so that others will read it and be attracted to Him. He grips us firmly, securing us in place—the place where He wants us to serve Him. He guides us and points us to the people around us who need to hear His Story. He gives us confidence and boldness, liberating us from our fears and self-doubts. And He beckons those who hunger to hear His Story, bringing them across our path so that our stories can collide with their stories, so that God's Story can go forth with *power*.

"OKAY, GOD, I HEAR YOU!"

Chris Humphries did not claim to be a Christian. Every once in a while, when he had a problem or a big decision to make, he would talk it over with God. He was like so many postmodern people—a deist, with a vague sense that there was Someone out there somewhere. But a Christian? Not Chris.

Then something came into Chris's life that upset his equilibrium: a prison. It was the old debtor's prison in the historic black section of Atlanta, not far from Atlanta Stadium. It had been closed and abandoned for sixty years. But then Chris heard that a group of Christians were renovating it to convert it into affordable housing for the poor.

As one of Atlanta's leading commercial contractors, imbued with a deep streak of civic pride, Chris found the project interesting. He followed the progress of the renovation in the papers. He drove by the former prison a couple of times, just to look at the massive vacant building. But, of course, the project had nothing to do with him, because those were Christians doing the renovating—and Chris was not a Christian.

Coincidentally, several of his friends suggested on various occasions that Chris should get involved with the project. He laughed it off. "That debtor's prison project is some sort of Christian thing," he said. "That's not for me."

The final straw came when Chris went to visit his foot doctor for an ingrown nail. The doctor—who was Jewish—said, "Chris, have you heard what they're doing down at the old debtor's prison? You know, that's just the kind of project you should get involved in."

At that point, Chris figured somebody was trying to tell him something. He decided to ask God what he should do.

Sometimes when Chris had a big decision to make, he would go to a monastery in Conyers, east of Atlanta, and pray. So he drove there late one December evening—but when he arrived, the monastery was closed. The brothers had all gone to bed. Chris was ticked off. It was as if God had closed up shop!

Driving back to Atlanta on Interstate 20, he followed a route that happened to take him right past the former prison. Just as he was passing the prison, he saw a light—*literally!* At exactly that moment, right before Chris's eyes, a huge Christmas tree lit up on top of the prison! It was like a sign from God! Chris later learned that a group of Christians had gathered at the prison to sing Christmas carols and light the huge Christmas tree.

When Chris saw that tree light up, he responded, "Okay, God, I hear You!" The next morning he called Bob Lupton, the director of the project, and said, "You don't know me, but I think I'm supposed to have something to do with the debtor's prison. I know this is a Christian project, and I'm no Christian, but I think I'm supposed to *run* that project."

The net-net of the story is that Chris took on the job as a full-time volunteer. He brought a group of building contractors together, and the old debtor's prison is now Glen Castle—a Christian residential community, a fellowship of the Holy Spirit that offers low-cost housing and social services for the needy, as well as a place of worship. Many people are coming to Christ at Glen Castle. And what's more, through the process of heading up that project, Chris Humphries has been changed. He has merged his story with the Story of God. In the process of giving leadership to the Glen Castle project, Chris has given God leadership over his life.

The story of Chris Humphries is the story of how the Holy Spirit arranged the events and influences in his life to move him to the place God wanted him to be. It is the story of the Holy Spirit drawing a man into community with Christians and into fellowship with Himself. Today, Chris Humphries has a story to tell. A story about a vision—a vision that transformed his life.

That is the attractive power of Christian community, of the fellowship of the Holy Spirit. Our community is a living apologia (an argument or justification) for the Christian faith. The modern apologia—the intellectual arguments of thinkers such as Francis Schaeffer, C. S. Lewis, Josh McDowell, and Os Guinness—may be brilliant, logical, and intellectually convincing, but the *post*modern mind is not as interested in modern logic and empirical evidence, as the modern mind once was. Today, the most soundly reasoned apologetics often are met with, "So what? Even if you've proved your case, it has no relevance to me." Remember, we are living in an age of deconstructionism, when logic and the meaning of words are no longer respected. We live in an age when people no longer ask, "What do you think?" but "How do you feel?" Or they may just say, "You have your truth, and I have mine."

So what is the most convincing apologia for a postmodern world? *Christian community.* That is the one proof that even deconstructionist, feelings-oriented, postmodern people cannot shrug off. When people see Christians living in deep fellowship with God the Father, with God the Son, with God the Holy Spirit, *and with each other*, they will be convinced that our Story is true. In our Lord's high priestly prayer before He went to the cross, He asked that His followers "may be one, Father, just as you are in me and I am in you. May they also be in us so that the world may believe that you have sent me."[13] Our best witness to the truth of the Story of God is our *oneness*, our *community*, our deep *fellowship* with one another in the Holy Spirit.

WHAT IF . . . ?

Now that Ben and Judith have been touched by the Story of God, what about Darrell?

If people like Darrell are to be changed by the gospel, they need to see that God is active in the lives of people today, that He is moving events and people. They need to see Christians experiencing fellowship with each other and with God. They need to see Christians living in reliance upon the power of the Spirit, even in times of weakness, hardship, and grief.

What would happen if the church truly became "a fellowship of the Holy Spirit"? If Christians opened up their lives, allowing nonbelievers to see the active, empowering, comforting presence of God's Spirit?

What would happen in the life of someone like Darrell?

CHAPTER FOURTEEN

STORY:
A New Story Begins

THE STORY GOES ON . . . ATLANTA, JULY 1996
Judith took Darrell's advice and tried the upside-down apple pie with cinnamon ice cream (she declared it "absolutely *mar*velous"), while Ben had a piece of "seriously chocolate cake" (since giving up his three-pack-a-day Camels habit, Ben had become something of a chocaholic).

"Well, Darrell," said Ben, "you said you had some news that'll knock our socks off—and I think I can guess what it is."

"Me, too," said Judith. "Ben's found a new home with God, and I'm on my way home, so I'll bet our friend Darrell is about to tell us—"

"That's right," said Darrell, grinning. "I've committed my life to Jesus Christ, too. It was all I could do to keep from blurting it out while the two of you were telling your stories. I came here thinking, *So much has happened to me in the past four years. I want to share it with Ben and Judith. I want them to know God the same way I've gotten to know Him!* And now I find out all three of us have been on parallel paths these past four years. It's amazing!"

"It gives me goose bumps!" added Judith, her eyes alight. "Tell us your story, Darrell!"

"I came back from Barcelona and finished my studies at UCLA. After that injury, I knew my Olympic career was in the past, so I buckled down, finished my law degree, and landed a job with a firm here in Atlanta. One of the partners in the firm was handling the legal work for the Olympic Organizing Committee, and he passed a lot of the grunt work—you know, the apprentice-level stuff—on to me. I was averaging over eighty hours a week for so-so pay, but I loved every minute of it. I wasn't a runner anymore, but I got to be a part—even if a small, behind-the-scenes part—of another Olympiad.

"I got to know a lot of the Olympic Committee staffers, and one of them—a fella named Greg—kept asking me to visit a men's Bible study he was involved in. I put him off and put him off. I didn't want to hurt the guy's feelings, but I sure didn't want to spend a lot of time doing religious stuff with a bunch of church people. Well, one weekend, Greg invited me to go with him and the other guys in the group on a camping trip up around Kennesaw Mountain. I thought, *Okay, let's go ahead and get this out of the way, and maybe he won't ask me anymore.* So I went. Problem was, I had a great time!

"Turns out these guys were a lot of fun—not a bunch of religious nerds like I expected. I'd been keeping up a really hectic pace at the firm, so it was the first time in months I'd taken a weekend to relax. The first night, they cooked steaks over the campfire and chatted about their work, their families, the upcoming Summer Games—and then they started talking about God. At first, I thought, *Uh-oh. What do I say? Should I shine these guys on and act religious so as to avoid any hassles? Or should I just tell them I'm an agnostic and wait for the preachin' to commence?* Well, I decided to be honest. When it came around to me, I just told 'em flat out, 'Look, guys, I don't believe in God.'

"Well, that didn't bother them at all. They didn't preach at me or tell me I was going to hell. They talked about what God was doing in their lives, but they didn't ram it down my throat.

Eventually, the conversation sorta turned around to other things—but I couldn't stop thinking about all the things they had said. I didn't realize it then, but I was going through something called 'the conviction of the Holy Spirit.' God was whispering to me, nudging me. He wouldn't let go of me, wouldn't let me stop thinking and wondering about Him.

"Before that camping trip, I used to be kind of wary around Greg. I liked him, he was a nice guy and all that—but I knew he was, quote, 'religious,' unquote, and I was afraid he might try to convert me. But that camping trip really changed my mind."

"How so?" asked Judith.

"Spending a weekend with those guys, I sensed something in their lives that I wanted, but didn't have. I could see that these guys had a real sense of *belonging* together—and yet I didn't feel like I was on the outside looking in. They accepted me as if I belonged, too. I had never felt that before. I know what that feeling is now, although I didn't know then. The early Christians called it *koinonia*."

"What does that mean?" asked Judith.

"It means 'fellowship,'" Ben piped up. "The fellowship of the Holy Spirit." He put his hands together, interlacing the fingers in a tight grip. "It's like these two hands of mine, pressed together into a single unit. *Koinonia* happens when Christians bond together like this—caring for each other, sharing together, becoming involved in each other's lives. My friend Don explained it to me at Bible study last week. Darrell, that's what you saw in these guys when you went on that camping trip, wasn't it? Real *koinonia*—fellowship in the Holy Spirit?"

"Yeah!" said Darrell. "That's it exactly! I was really attracted to these people because they had this *koinonia* thing and I didn't. Well, time passed, and Greg and his wife, Nikole, invited me over a lot. I joined the men's Bible study. And the more I got to know Greg and Nikki and the guys in the Bible study, the more amazed I became. I saw that these people were not only involved in a close Christian fellowship, but they were giving a lot of hours to help other people—people they didn't even know.

"You see, it's an inner-city church, a mixture of poor, inner-city people and middle-class African-American professionals. A lot of these upwardly mobile professionals could have said, 'I've made it. I've found the American dream. I never have to go back to the old neighborhood again.' But these people didn't just make their escape from the 'hood, they're still involved! They give leadership to that church, and they're making a difference in the inner city of Atlanta. Just look at my friends, Greg and Nikki. They have been volunteering with a project that remodeled the old debtor's prison and turned it into low-income housing, and the guys in the Bible study group donated tons of time to an inner-city ministry.

"But what impressed me most about Greg and Nikki was the kind of power God seemed to give them in a really heartbreaking situation. They have this little daughter, Julia. She's six years old, cute as a button—but she's very sick with leukemia. I'd be visiting in their home, and I'd remember how my mother's cancer killed my faith when I was a boy. And I'd think, *Wow! How can these people do this? How can they have a strong faith in God while their little girl is living under this awful shadow?* I could tell they had something inside them—a peace, a joy—that had nothing whatever to do with their circumstances. And it really made me wonder: *Where does that power come from?* Man, I was baffled.

"Then I saw how their friends from church gathered around them and took care of them. They did a lot of practical stuff for Greg and Nikole—baby-sitting, mowing the yard, fixing the fence— so the two of them could spend time with each other, or devote more time to Julia. I had always thought of church as a *building*. But this church was more like a *family*. I mean, these people *really* loved each other!

"As I watched this, I kept asking myself, *How do they do it?* One explanation kept coming to my mind: There's a Spirit in those people. A real, living Spirit. I had no choice but to believe it and accept it. So one night, as I was sitting at dinner with Greg and Nikki, I said to Greg, 'Tell me how I can have what you've got.' And Greg explained it to me and prayed with me. That was about a year ago."

"Has it made a difference in your life?" asked Judith.

"Has it made a difference!" Darrell exclaimed, his eyes shining. "Let me tell you something: These past few months, I've been under a mountain of pressure, handling legal work for the Olympic Committee. People have no idea what goes on behind the scenes to put on one of these international dog-and-pony shows. Long hours, short deadlines, people screamin' at you if things don't get done on time. I don't know how I could have gotten through these last few weeks before the Games. In fact, a friend of mine *didn't* get through it."

"What do you mean?" asked Ben.

"This guy in my office, a new attorney like me, was having a hard time handling the pressure. He started smoking methamphetamine. That stuff makes you euphoric, energetic, helps you keep going when you're fatigued. There's a real temptation to use stuff like that when you're putting in ninety-, hundred-hour weeks, and this guy, Cliff, not only succumbed to it, but he offered me some of his stuff. A year ago, I might have smoked it too, to help me deal with the pressure. And I also might have ended up dead like Cliff. 'Meth heads' tend to get very weird—agitated, paranoid, really hair-triggered. About six weeks ago, Cliff called the office, said he wasn't coming in to work that day, then he put down the phone and blew his brains out.

Judith gasped.

"Oh man . . . ," said Ben.

"If it hadn't been for God and my Christian friends getting me through the pressure and craziness," said Darrell with a deep sigh, "what happened to Cliff could have happened to me. I really believe that.

"And I'll tell you something else I believe. God is *real*. His Spirit is living in me. Judith, I'll keep praying for you. I know that God has a whole new life planned for you. And when the moment comes that you make that decision to commit your life to Him, I hope you'll call me. Instantly."

"Yeah," said Ben. "Me, too."

"I will," said Judith. "I promise I will."

"I've got a question for you two," said Darrell. "Could you both arrange to be in Atlanta after the Games are over?"

"Sure," said Ben. "In fact, my vacation starts the very next day."

"And I'll be here for another week," said Judith, "doing advance work for some upcoming stories on the Falcons. Why do you ask?"

"Because that Sunday night after the Olympics," said Darrell, "I have a little celebration that I'd like you both to be a part of."

"A celebration?" said Ben.

"What kind of celebration?" asked Judith.

"My baptism," said Darrell. "Right after that flame goes out in the stadium Saturday night, a new flame goes on Sunday morning—in me!"

THE STORY GOES ON FOREVER

Here our narrative of Ben and Judith and Darrell comes to a close. But their stories go on and on. These three people are merging their stories with the changeless-yet-ever-changing Story of God. That Story goes on forever, weaving its way through countless human lives, countless human stories. We are all part of that great narrative, as we join our stories to His. And we *expand* that narrative as we call others to join their stories to His.

As Henri Nouwen has so beautifully stated,

> I still believe deeply that our few years on this earth are part of a much larger event that stretches out beyond the boundaries of our birth and death. I think of it as a mission into time, a mission that is very exhilarating, and even exciting, mostly because the One who sent me on the mission is waiting for me to come home and *tell the story* of what I have learned.[1]

179

May the *grace* of our Lord Jesus Christ, and the *love* of God, and the *fellowship* of the Holy Spirit be with us all.

    And with Ben.

    And with Judith.

    And with Darrell.

NOTES

Chapter One—The Story of God
1. 2 Corinthians 13:14.

Chapter Three—Toward 2000—and Beyond
1. Paul Johnson, *Modern Times: The World from the Twenties to the Eighties* (New York: Harper & Row, 1983), page 48.

Chapter Four—"Tell Us a Story"
1. Paul Davies, *God and the New Physics* (New York: Simon & Schuster, 1983), page ix.
2. Quoted by Richard D. Meisner in "Universe—the Ultimate Artifact?" *Analog*, April 1987, page 63.
3. Diogenes Allen, *Christian Belief in a Post-Modern World* (Louisville, KY: Westminster/John Knox Press, 1989), page 4.
4. To protect the security of missionaries and national Christians involved in this story, I cannot name the country.
5. Ephesians 5:15-16.
6. Luke 10:4.

Chapter Six—A Generation in Search of Fatherhood

1. 2 Corinthians 13:14, emphasis added.
2. Hebrews 11:6.
3. David Lehman, *Signs of the Times: Deconstruction and the Fall of Paul de Man* (New York: Poseidon Press, 1992), pages 40-41.
4. Judith Weinraub, "The New Theology: Sheology," *Washington Post* (April 28, 1992). Retrieved on CompuServe Executive News Service.

Chapter Seven—An Old Story for a New Age

1. Bilquis Sheikh, "I Dare to Call Him Father," from *The Lord of the Journey: A Reader in Christian Spirituality*, ed. by Roger Pooley and Philip Seddon (London: Collins Liturgical Publications, 1986), pages 90-91.
2. Luke 15:1-2.
3. Matthew 5:16.
4. Matthew 5:43-45.
5. Matthew 6:8,26.

Chapter Nine—The Story Made Visible

1. Philippians 3:12, freely paraphrased by author.
2. 2 Corinthians 4:6-7.
3. 1 Timothy 1:14.
4. Ephesians 2:8.
5. Titus 2:11.
6. 2 Corinthians 8:9.
7. Acts 26:14-16,19, emphasis added.

Chapter Ten—A Touch of Grace

1. See Acts 9:10-19.
2. Colossians 4:6.
3. Luke 4:22.
4. Acts 4:33.
5. Matthew 9:9-13.
6. Matthew 5:11.

Chapter Twelve—In Search of Power and Community
1. Psalm 63:1.
2. Matthew 28:18-19.
3. Acts 1:4, emphasis added.
4. Acts 1:8, author's paraphrase.
5. Acts 10:28, author's paraphrase.
6. Author's paraphrase of Peter's words in Acts 10:26-28.

Chapter Thirteen—The "Five-Finger Exercise"
1. Luke 11:20, emphasis added.
2. Matthew 12:28, emphasis added.
3. Acts 2:37.
4. Acts 11:21.
5. Acts 2:38.
6. See Matthew 5:13.
7. See 2 Corinthians 2:14-15.
8. Psalm 8:3.
9. See Exodus 31:18.
10. 2 Corinthians 3:3.
11. 2 Corinthians 3:17.
12. Exodus 31:1-5.
13. John 17:21.

Epilogue—The Story Goes On Forever
1. Henri Nouwen, *Life of the Beloved* (New York: Crossroad Publishing, 1992), page 180.

AUTHOR

Dr. Leighton Ford is President of Leighton Ford Ministries, which focuses on raising up younger leaders to spread the message of Christ worldwide. He has spoken face to face to millions of people in thirty-five countries, on every continent. He served as associate evangelist and later vice president of the Billy Graham Evangelistic Association. For many years Dr. Ford was featured as the alternate speaker to Billy Graham on the Hour of Decision broadcast, and broadcast his own daily TV and radio spots in the United States, Canada, and Australia.

Dr. Ford's book *Transforming Leadership* (1991) received the 1990 Two Hungers Award, which recognized his contributions to addressing the physical and spiritual hungers of people around the world. In 1985 Dr. Ford was selected Clergyman of the Year by Religious Heritage of America and as Presbyterian Preacher of the Year by the National Presbyterian Center. *TIME Magazine* singled him out as being "among the most influential preachers of an active gospel." He is Honorary Life Chairman of the Lausanne Committee for World Evangelization, having served from 1976 to 1992 as chairman of this international body of Christian leaders. He currently serves as a board member for World Vision U.S., the Duke University Comprehensive Cancer Center, and Gordon-Conwell Theological Seminary.

Leighton Ford lives in Charlotte, North Carolina, with his wife, Jean. They have a married daughter, Deborah, and a married son, Kevin, who is in full-time ministry. Their older son, Sandy, died after heart surgery in November 1981.

Other Books by Leighton Ford

The Christian Persuader (Harper & Row, 1966)
Letters to a New Christian (World Wide Publications, 1967)
One Way to Change the World (Harper & Row, 1970)
New Man . . . New World (Word, 1972)
Good News Is For Sharing (David C. Cook, 1976)
Sandy: A Heart For God (InterVarsity, 1985)
Meeting Jesus (InterVarsity, 1988)
Transforming Leadership (InterVarsity, 1991)